PIANO | VOCAL | GUITAR

Sam Smith
Love Goes

ISBN 978-1-70512-800-8

Visit Hal Leonard Online at
www.halleonard.com

Contact us:
Hal Leonard
7777 West Bluemound Road
Milwaukee, WI 53213
Email: info@halleonard.com

In Europe, contact:
Hal Leonard Europe Limited
42 Wigmore Street
Marylebone, London, W1U 2RN
Email: info@halleonardeurope.com

In Australia, contact:
Hal Leonard Australia Pty. Ltd.
4 Lentara Court
Cheltenham, Victoria, 3192 Australia
Email: info@halleonard.com.au

YOUNG

Words and Music by SAM SMITH
and STEVE MAC

I wan-na be _____ wild _____ and young and

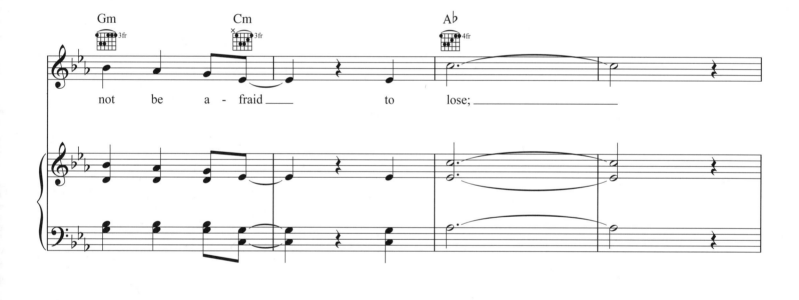

not be a-fraid _____ to lose; _____

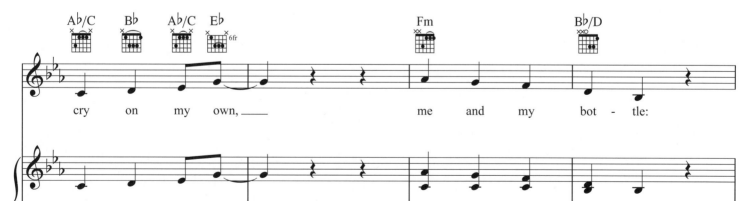

cry on my own, _____ me and my bot-tle:

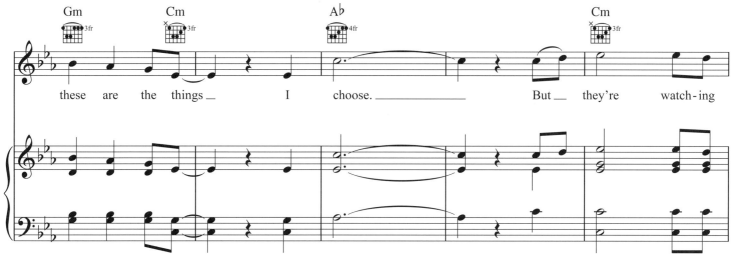

these are the things __ I choose. _____ But __ they're watch-ing

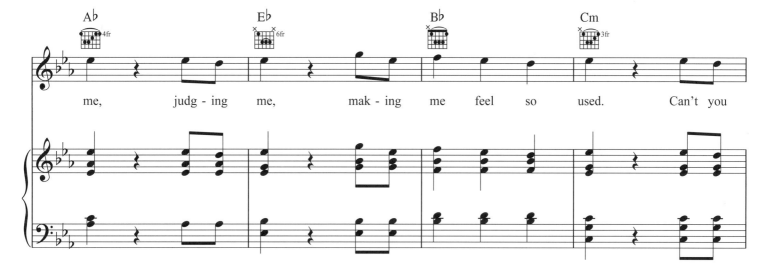

me, judg-ing me, mak-ing me feel so used. Can't you

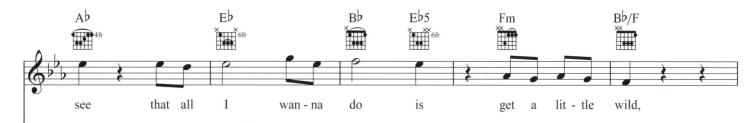

see that all I wan-na do is get a lit-tle wild,

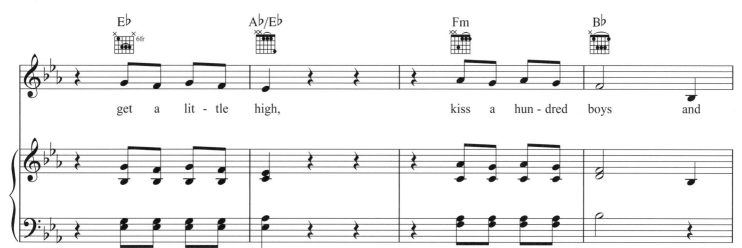

get a lit-tle high, kiss a hun-dred boys and

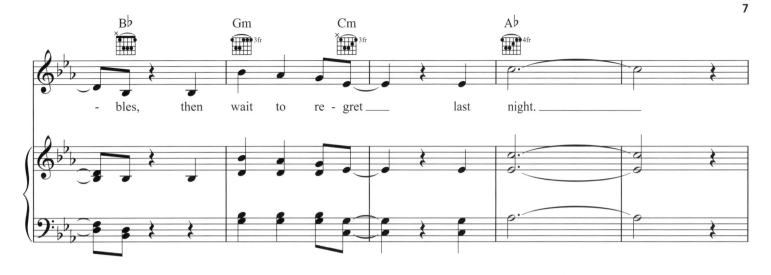

-bles, then wait to re - gret ___ last night. ___

My heav - y heart ___ pounds deep like a dag - ger, ___ 'cause

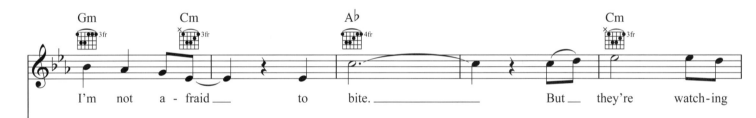

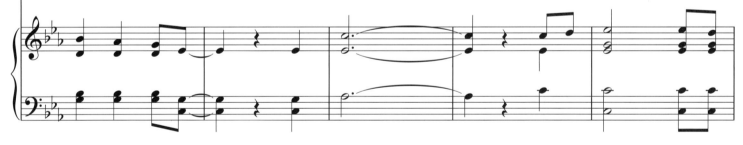

I'm not a - fraid ___ to bite. ___ But ___ they're watch - ing

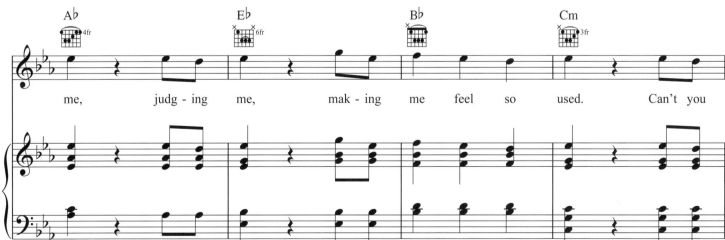

me, judg - ing me, mak - ing me feel so used. Can't you

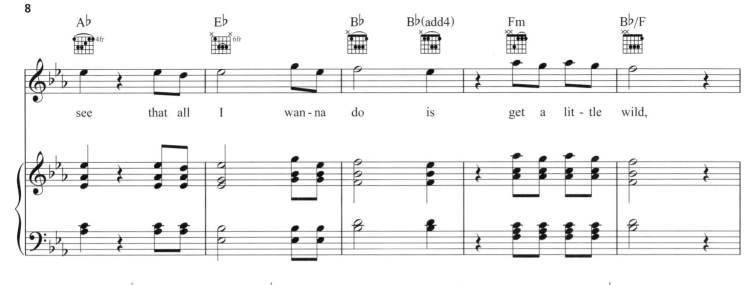

see that all I wan-na do is get a lit-tle wild,

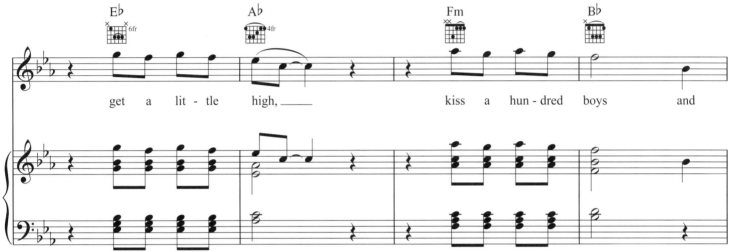

get a lit-tle high, _____ kiss a hun-dred boys and

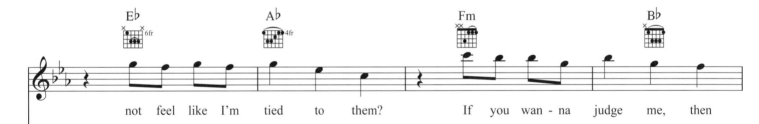

not feel like I'm tied to them? If you wan-na judge me, then

go and load the gun. _____ I've done noth-ing wrong; I'm

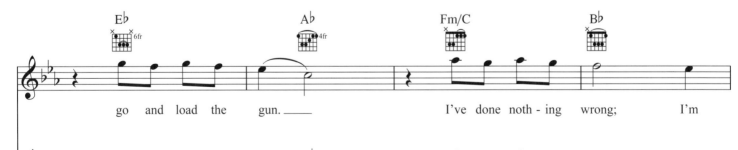

DIAMONDS

Words and Music by SAM SMITH,
OSCAR GORRES and SHELLBACK

* Recorded a half step higher.

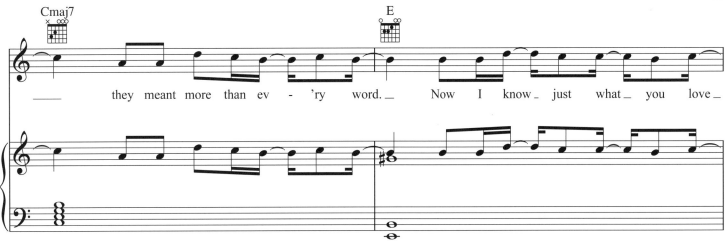

they meant more than ev - 'ry word. __ Now I know __ just what __ you love __

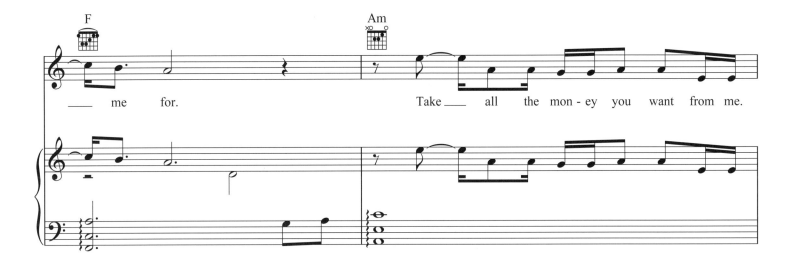

__ me for. Take __ all the mon - ey you want from me.

Hope __ you be - come what you want to be. Show __ me how lit - tle you care, how

lit - tle you care, how lit - tle you care. You __ dream of glit - ter and gold.

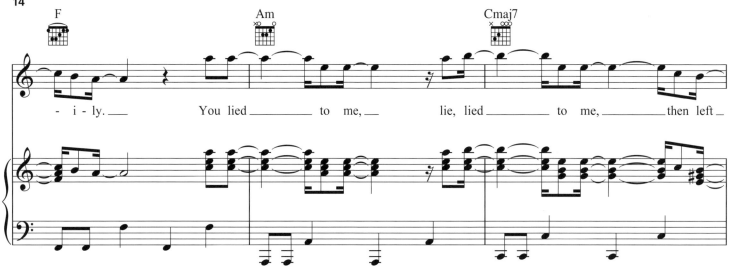

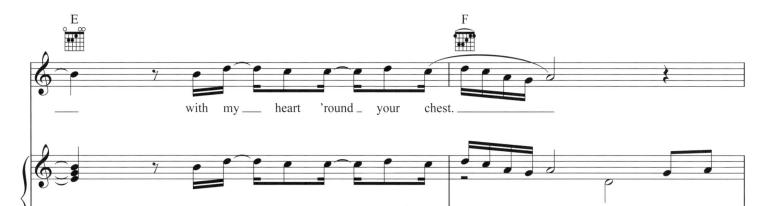

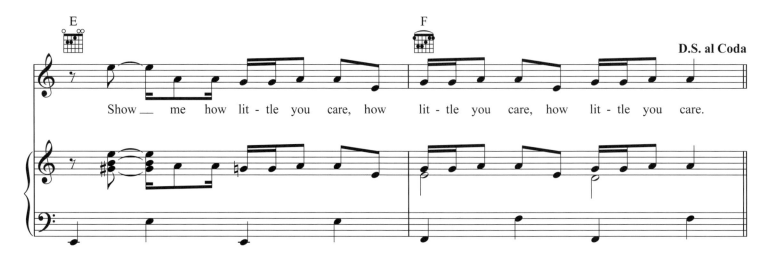

ANOTHER ONE

Words and Music by SAM SMITH,
NOONIE BAO and LINUS WIKLUND

Moderately fast

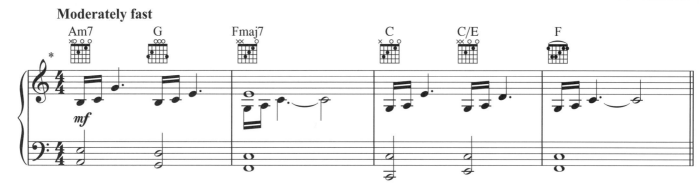

Oh, con-grat-u-la-tions: you found the one, you found the

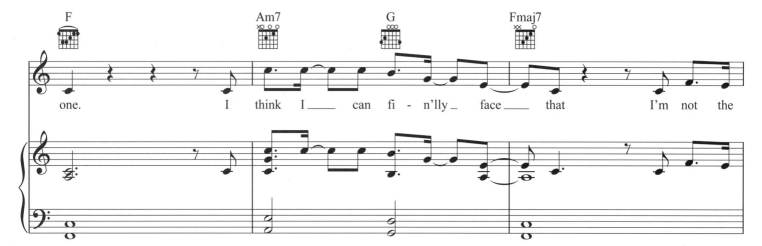

one. I think I___ can fi-n'lly___ face___ that I'm not the

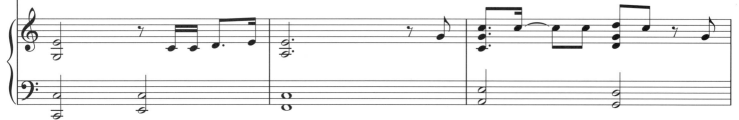

one, nev-er was the one. God, I dodged___ a bul-let, I

*Recorded a half step higher.

ran fast __ right through it. I love my - self too much __ to fight you. But

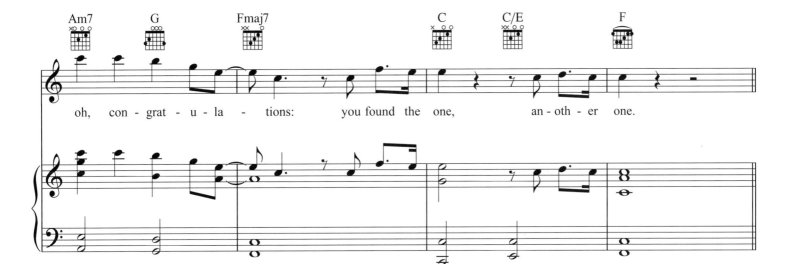

oh, con - grat - u - la - tions: you found the one, an - oth - er one.

You found the one, an - oth - er

one. Hon - est - ly I'm hap - py for you.

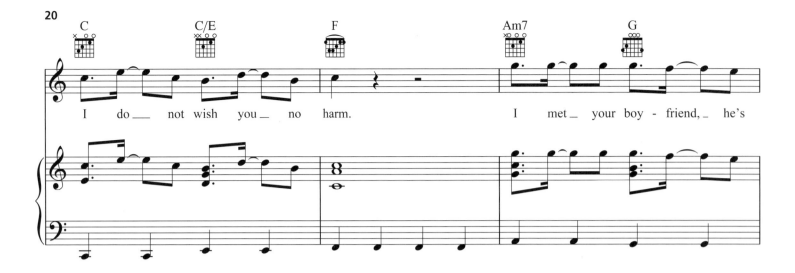

I do __ not wish you __ no harm. I met __ your boy - friend, __ he's

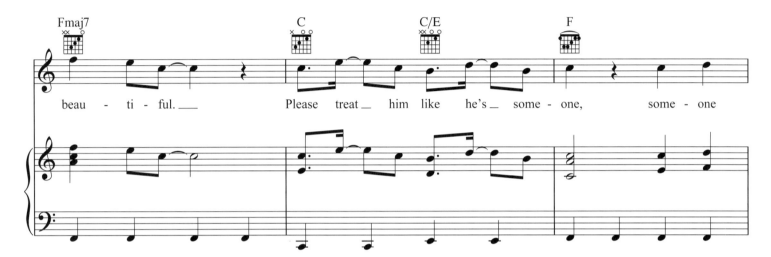

beau - ti - ful. __ Please treat __ him like he's __ some - one, some - one

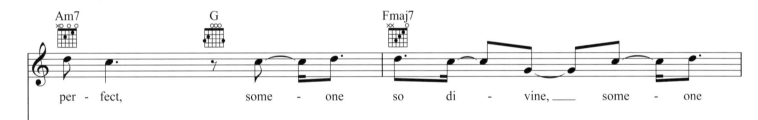

per - fect, some - one so di - vine, __ some - one

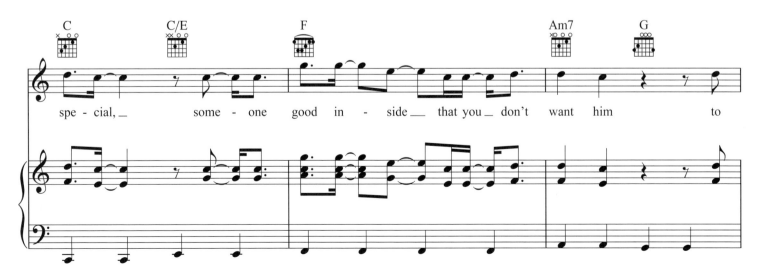

spe - cial, __ some - one good in - side __ that you __ don't want him to

hurt like ___ me.   Just please treat ___ him like he's ___ some -

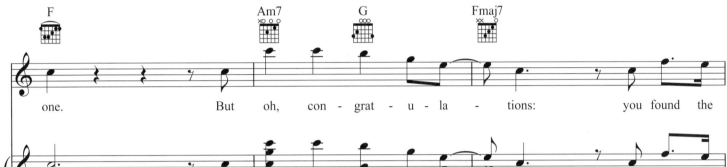

one.   But oh, con - grat - u - la - tions: you found the

one,   you found the one.   I think I ___ can fi - n'lly __ face _

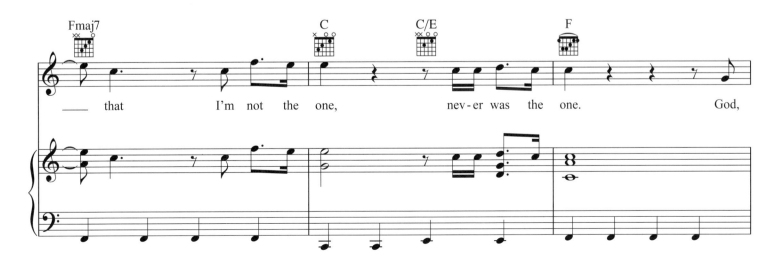

__ that   I'm not the one,   nev - er was the one.   God,

I dodged _ a bul - let, I ran fast __ right through it. I

love my - self too much _ to fight you. But oh, con - grat - u - la -

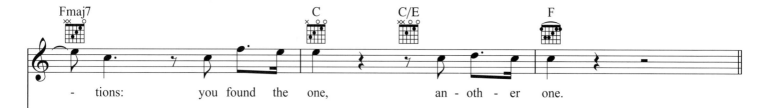

- tions: you found the one, an - oth - er one.

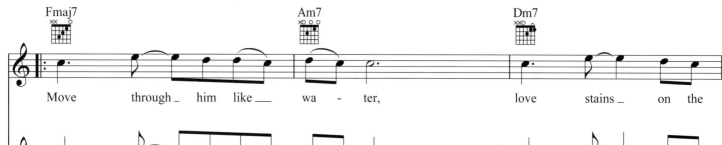

Move through _ him like __ wa - ter, love stains _ on the

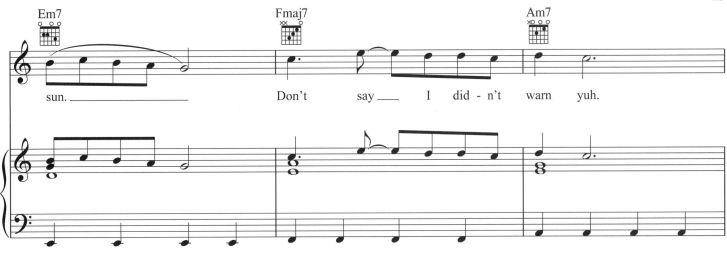

sun. _____ Don't say ___ I did-n't warn yuh.

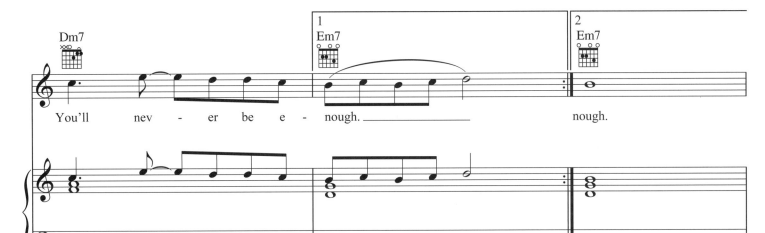

You'll nev - er be e - nough. _____ nough.

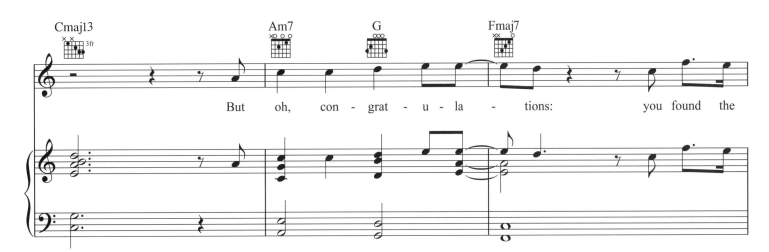

But oh, con - grat - u - la - tions: you found the

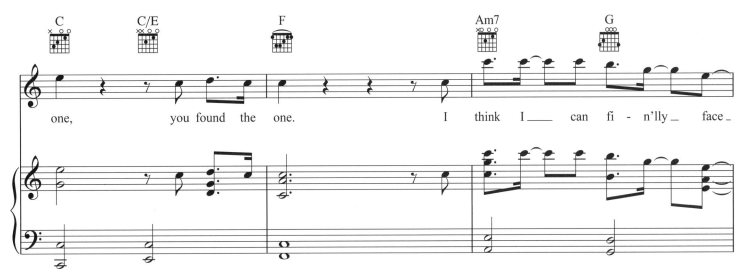

one, _____ you found the one. I think I ___ can fi - n'lly ___ face ___

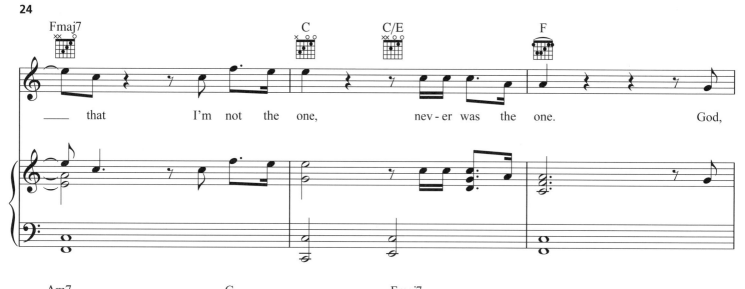

_____ that I'm not the one, nev-er was the one. God,

I dodged _ a bul - let, I ran fast _ right through it. I

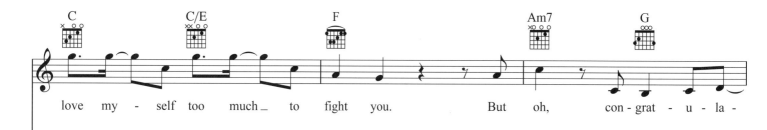

love my - self too much _ to fight you. But oh, con - grat - u - la -

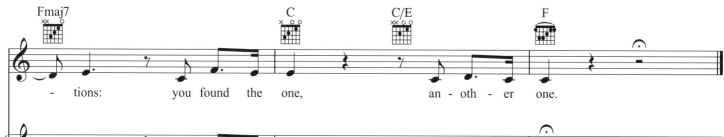

- tions: you found the one, an - oth - er one.

MY OASIS

Words and Music by SAM SMITH,
JAMES NAPIER and DAMINI OGULU

Keep think-ing that I'm see-ing wa-

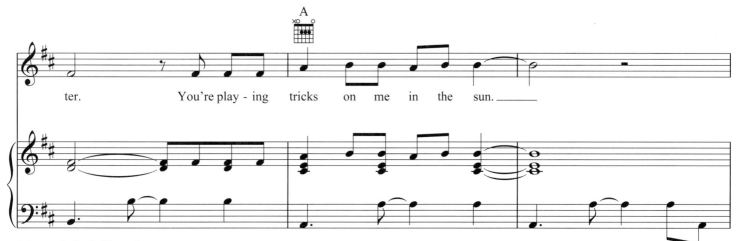

ter. You're play-ing tricks on me in the sun.

* Recorded a half step lower.

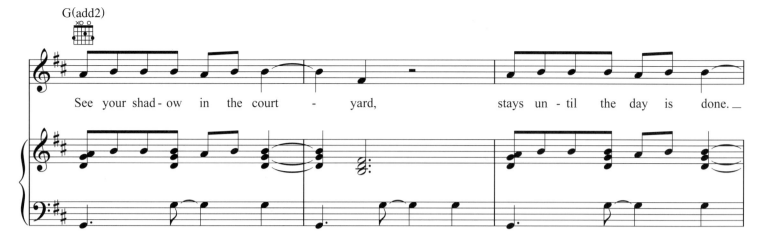

See your shad - ow in the court - yard, stays un - til the day is done.

___ The des - ert don't end, the rain ___ don't fall, and I can't pre -

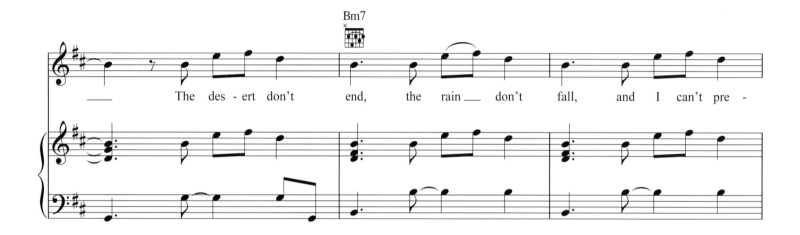

tend I don't want you all 'cause I want you all, _____

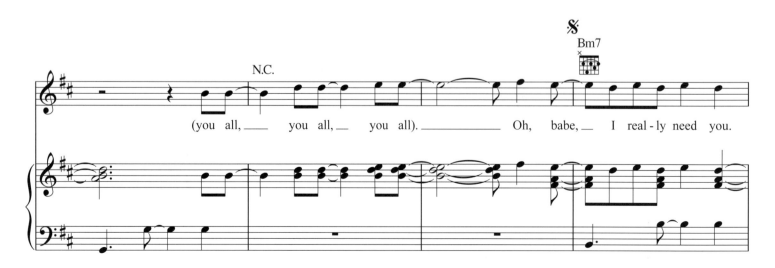

(you all, ___ you all, ___ you all). ___ Oh, babe, ___ I real - ly need you.

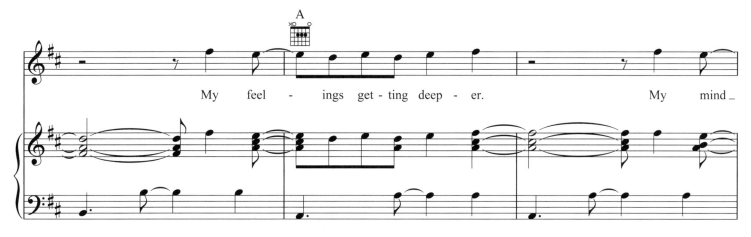

My feel - ings get - ting deep - er. My mind __

__ is in a free fall, _____ but there's noth - ing I can do when it

comes to you. You play __ with my e - mo - tions, I'm flow - ing like the o - cean. __

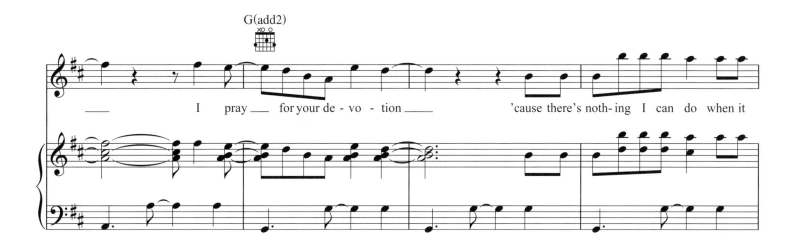

__ I pray __ for your de - vo - tion ____ 'cause there's noth - ing I can do when it

comes to you. _____ My o - a, my o - a, my o - a - sis. My o - a, my o -

a, my o - a - sis. My o - a, my o - a, my o - a - sis. There's noth - ing I can do when it

To Coda ⊕

comes to you. _____ Wait a min - ute, tell me why you're mov - ing like that. __ Na

you wey I choose, but you make it so hard. __ I gave you my heart, you're mak -

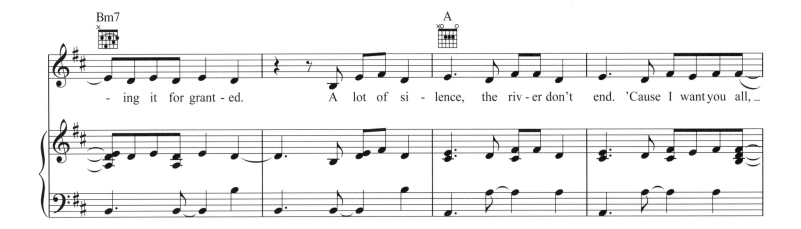

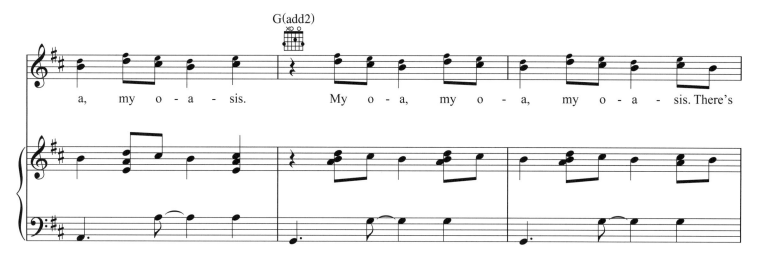

G(add2)

a, my o - a - sis. My o - a, my o - a, my o - a - sis. There's

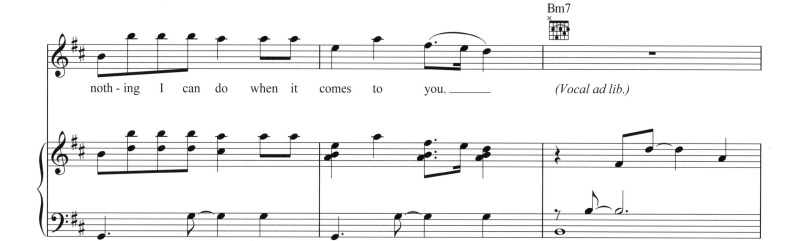

Bm7

noth - ing I can do when it comes to you. _____ *(Vocal ad lib.)*

A   G(add2)

SO SERIOUS

Words and Music by SAM SMITH,
NOONIE BAO and LINUS WIKLUND

Moderately, in 2

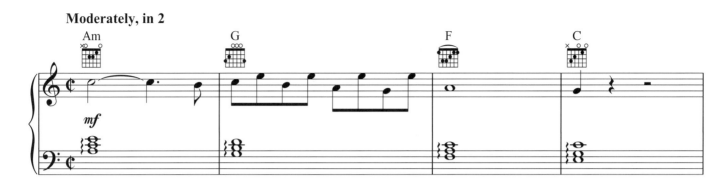

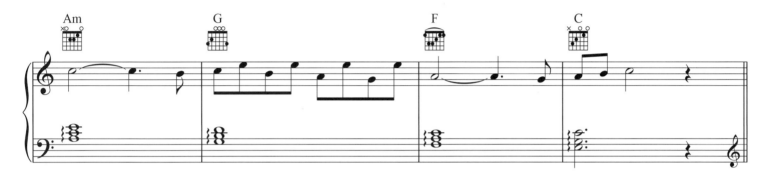

Put your hands in the air if you some-times ev-er get sad, like
I re-mem-ber last sum-mer in the cit-y, mak-ing plans, and you felt like

me.
mine.

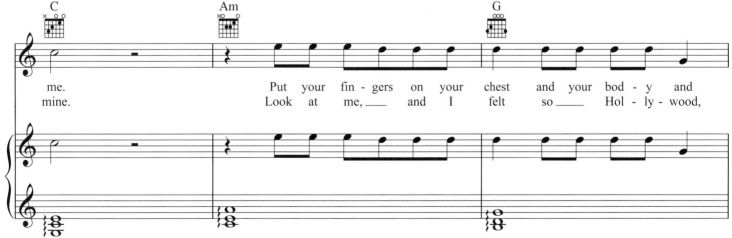

Put your fin-gers on your chest and your bod-y and
Look at me, and I felt so Hol-ly-wood,

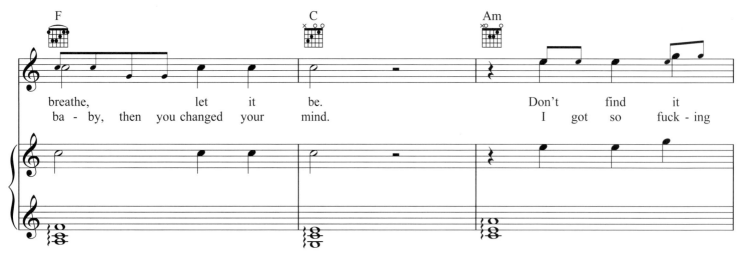

breathe,   let   it   be.   Don't   find   it
ba - by,   then   you changed   your   mind.   I   got   so   fuck - ing

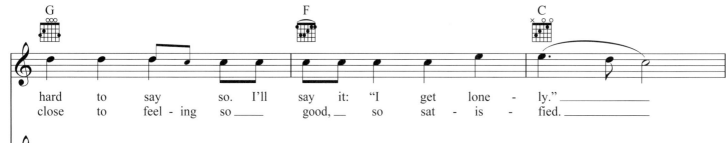

hard   to   say   so.   I'll   say   it: "I   get   lone - ly." _____
close   to   feel - ing   so ___   good, __   so   sat - is - fied. _____

Put   your hands   in   the   air   if   you some - times   ev - er   get   sad,   like
I   re - mem - ber   last ___   sum - mer   in   the   cit - ty,   mak - ing   plans, _   and   you   felt   like

me.   Sad   like   me. _____   Wait   pa - tient - ly _____
mine.   Felt   like   mine, _____   then   I   froze   in   time. _____

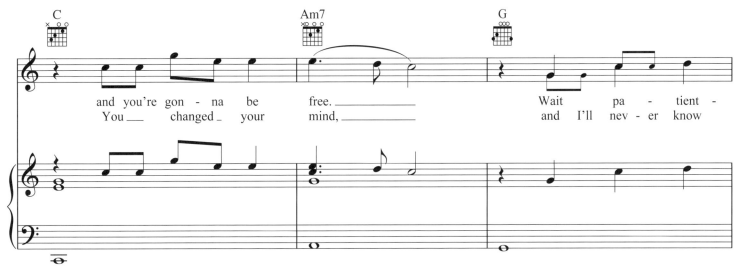

and you're gon - na be free. _____ Wait pa - tient -
You __ changed __ your mind, _____ and I'll nev - er know

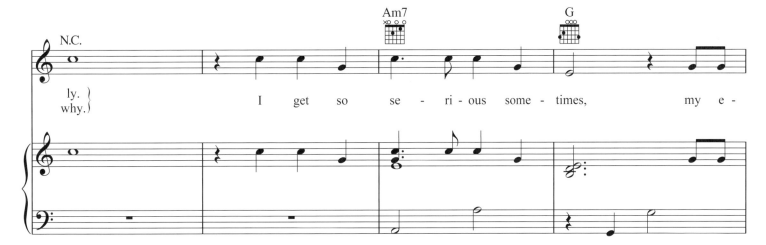

ly. }
why. } I get so se - ri - ous some - times, my e -

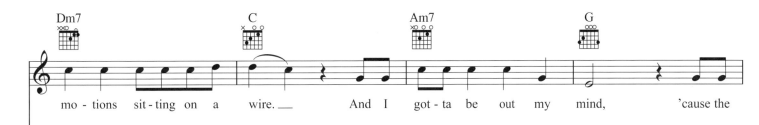

mo - tions sit - ting on a wire. __ And I got - ta be out my mind, 'cause the

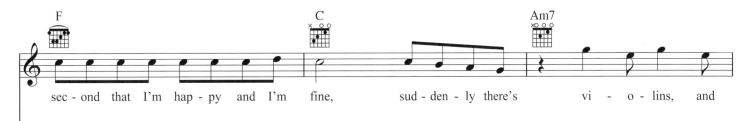

sec - ond that I'm hap - py and I'm fine, sud - den - ly there's vi - o - lins, and

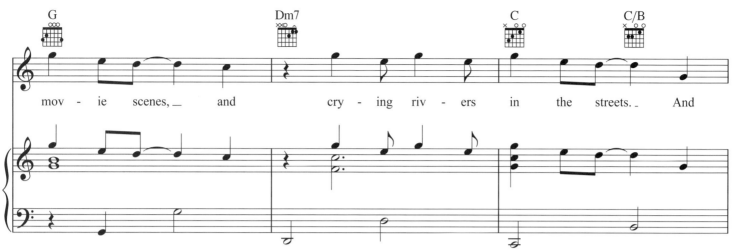

movie scenes, ___ and cry - ing riv - ers in the streets. ___ And

To Coda ⊕

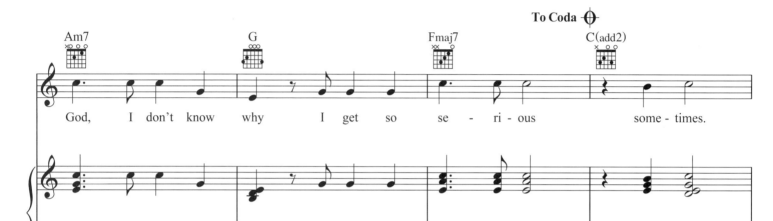

God, I don't know why I get so se - ri - ous some - times.

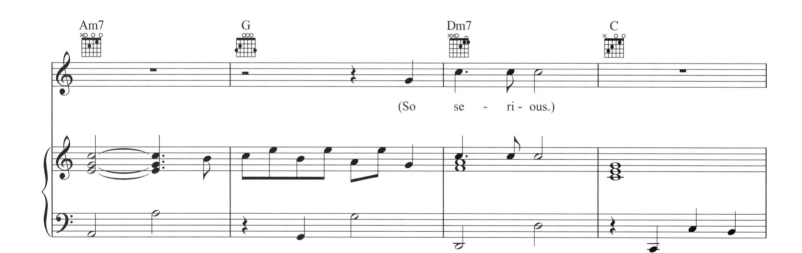

(So se - ri - ous.)

(So se - ri - ous some - times.

D.S. al Coda

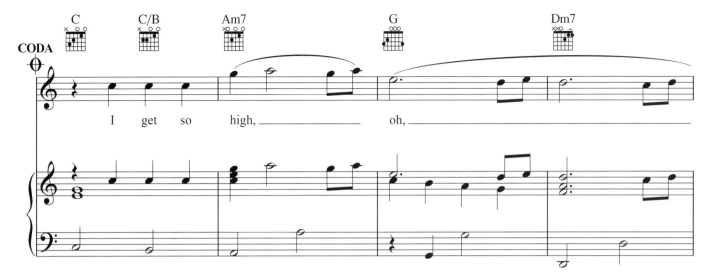

I get so high, _____ oh, _____

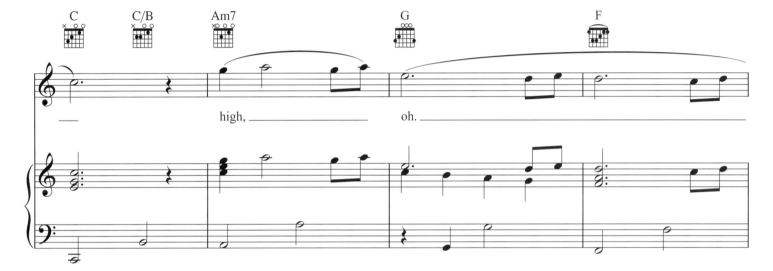

high, _____ oh. _____

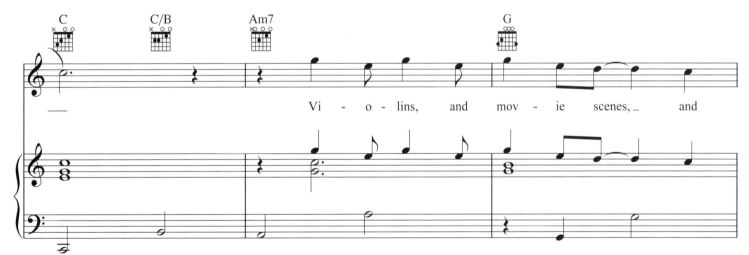

Vi - o - lins, and mov - ie scenes, _ and

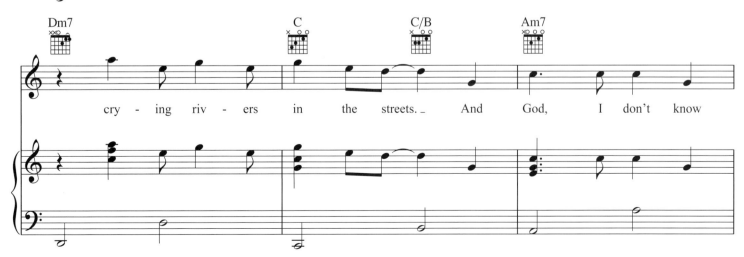

cry - ing riv - ers in the streets. _ And God, I don't know

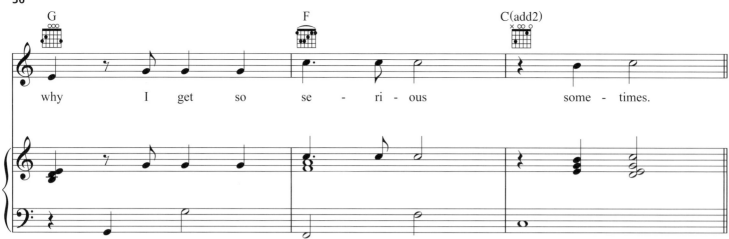

why I get so se - ri - ous some - times.

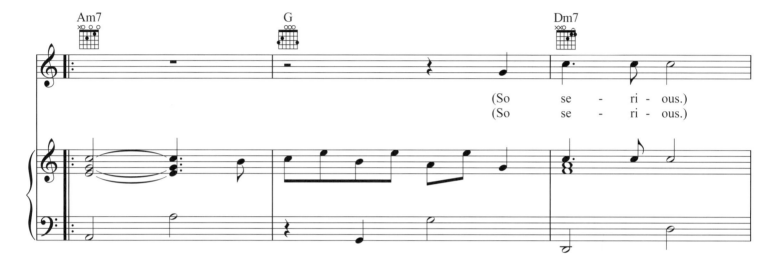

(So se - ri - ous.)
(So se - ri - ous.)

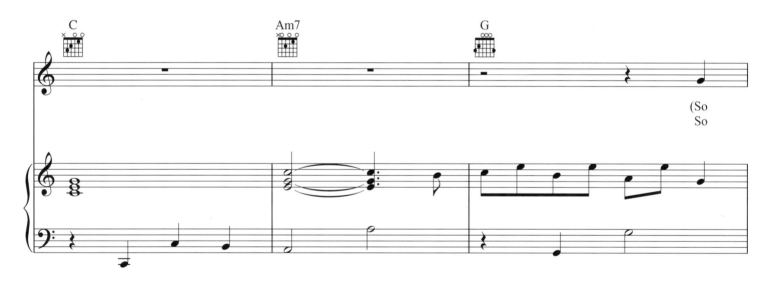

(So
So

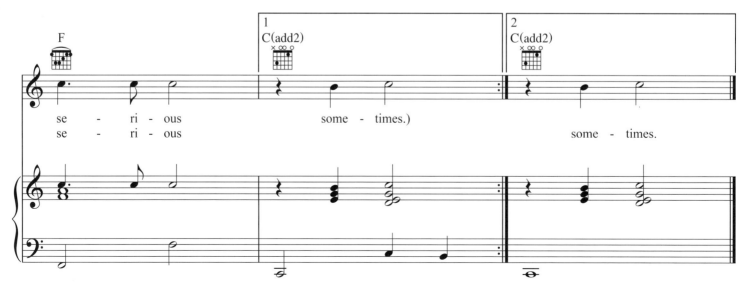

se - ri - ous some - times.)
se - ri - ous some - times.

DANCE
('Til You Love Someone Else)

Words and Music by SAM SMITH,
BEN ASH and AMY ALLEN

Moderately fast

Thought I bur-ied you__ and I,__ but I have dia-monds in__ my eyes.__ Such a bit-ter tear__ to cry.__ You're still ru-in-ing__ my life.__ I'm not o - ver it. I'm not o-

-ver it.　　　　I re-mem-ber ev-'ry taste.＿ If I

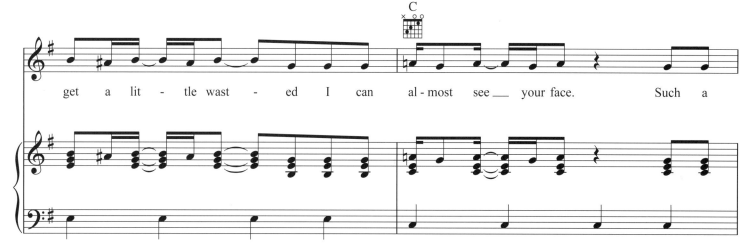

get a lit-tle wast-ed I can al-most see＿ your face.　　Such a

dark and lone-ly place.＿ I'm not o-ver it.

Some-one get＿ me o-ver it.　　　　And con-fide＿

in me. ___ Wrap your arms ___ a - round ___ me, ba -

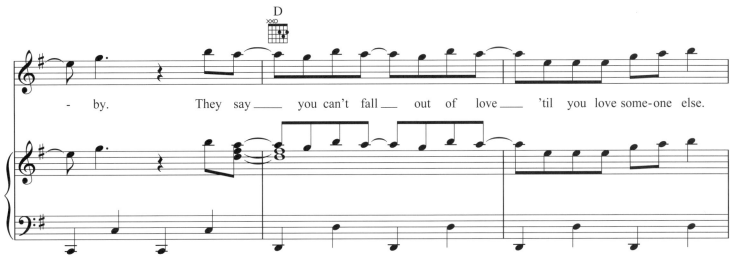

- by. They say ___ you can't fall ___ out of love ___ 'til you love some-one else.

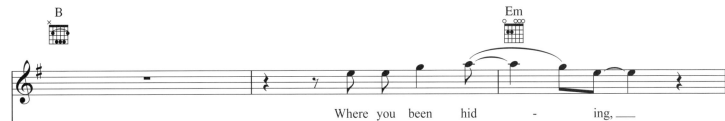

Where you been hid - ing, ___

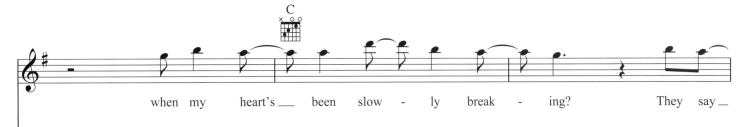

when my heart's ___ been slow - ly break - ing? They say ___

Em

get the way_ you move_ me. Try and drown you in_ the mu - sic. Hold my

C

breath and close_ my eyes._ Try to drag you out_ my mind._ Still not o -

D   B

- ver it.   Some-one get_ me o - ver it._

D.S. al Coda

And con - fide_

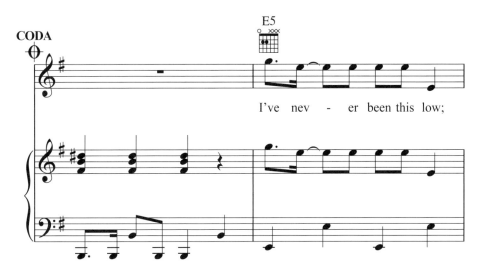

CODA

E5

I've nev - er been this low;

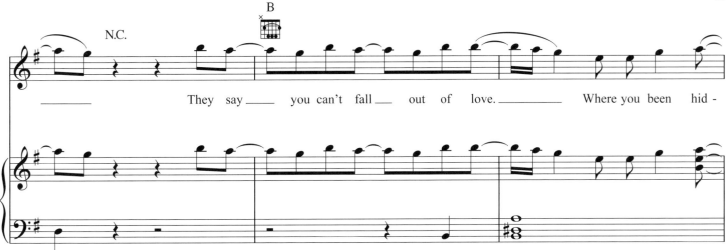

They say ___ you can't fall ___ out of love. ___ Where you been hid -

- ing, ___ when my heart's ___ been slow - ly break -

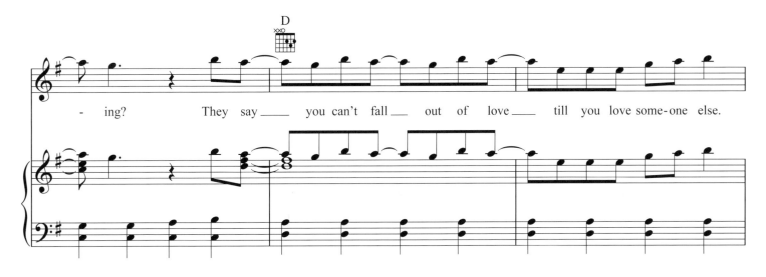

- ing? They say ___ you can't fall ___ out of love ___ till you love some-one else.

Guess ___ I'll dance.

Guess _ I'll dance. _____ They say _

_____ you can't fall _ out of love ___ till you love some-one else.

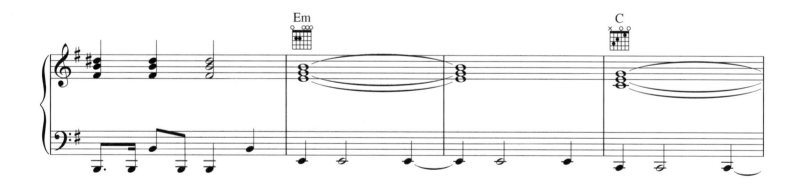

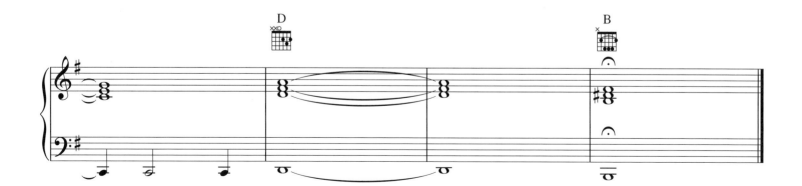

FOR THE LOVER THAT I LOST

Words and Music by SAM SMITH,
MIKKEL ERIKSEN, TOR HERMANSEN
and JAMES NAPIER

Recorded a half step lower.

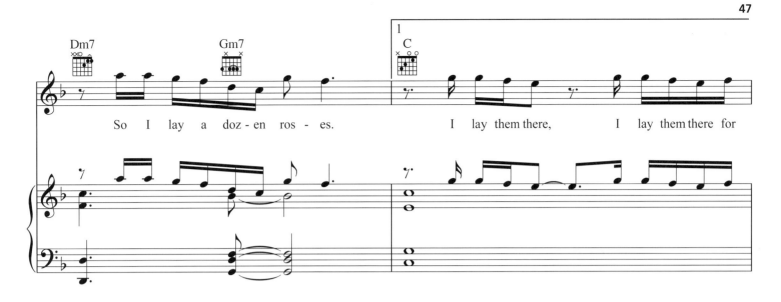

So I lay a doz - en ros - es. I lay them there, I lay them there for

you. _____

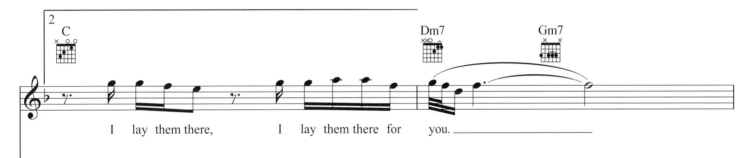

I lay them there, I lay them there for you. _____

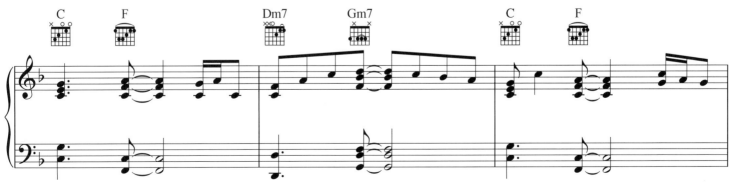

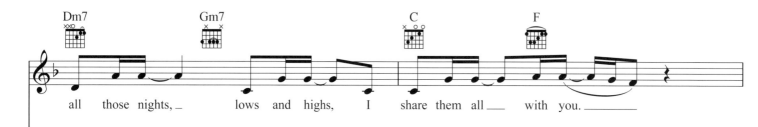

BREAKING HEARTS

Words and Music by SAM SMITH
and JAMES NAPIER

You went cold. You got caught. You ex-ceed-ed my
Went so far down this road. I felt de-pres-sion deep

dark-est thought. A poi-son chal-ice, thorn in my side.
in my soul. Drug-fueled fights, ride your lows and highs: We

I'm so numb from your lies.
played it all out till we died. While you were bus-y break-ing hearts,

break-ing.

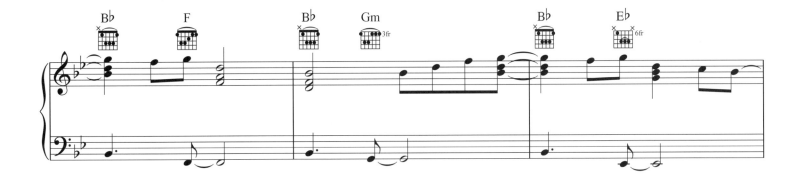

While you were bus-y break-ing hearts, ____

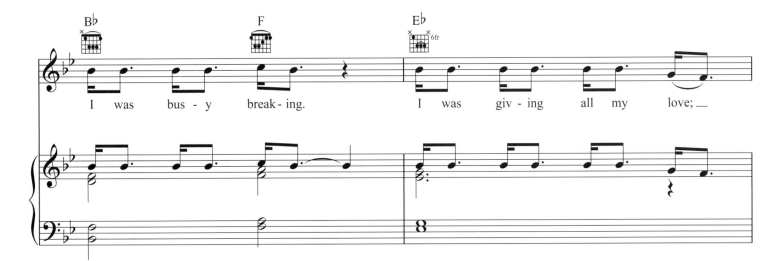

I was bus-y break-ing. I was giv-ing all my love; ____

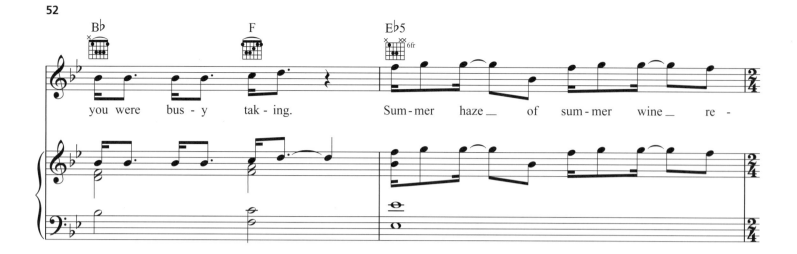

you were bus - y tak - ing. Sum - mer haze __ of sum - mer wine __ re -

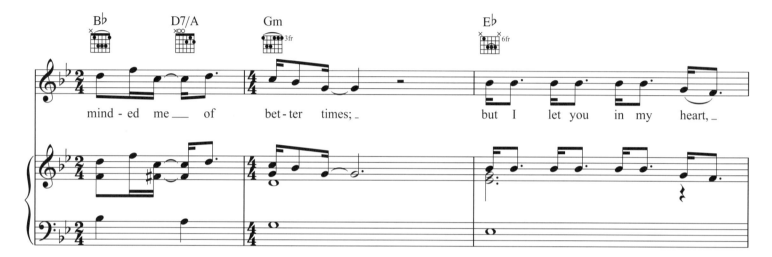

mind - ed me __ of bet - ter times; __ but I let you in my heart, __

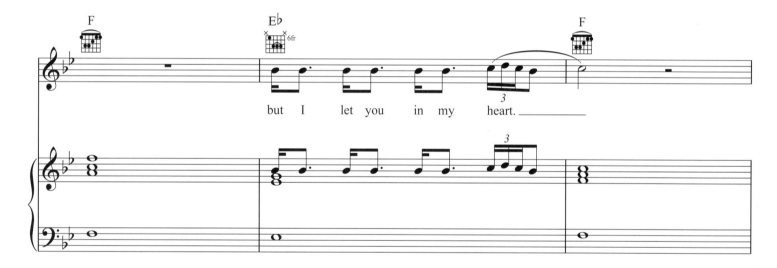

but I let you in my heart. ___

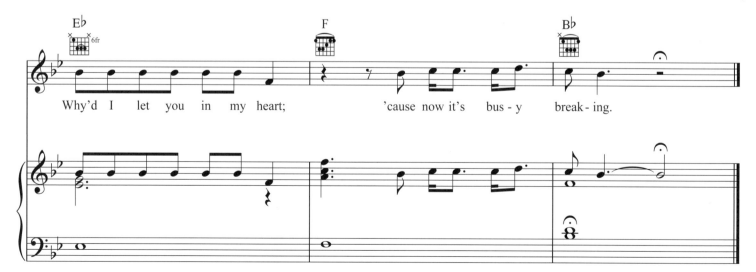

Why'd I let you in my heart; 'cause now it's bus - y break - ing.

FORGIVE MYSELF

Words and Music by SAM SMITH,
MIKKEL ERIKSEN, TOR HERMANSEN
and JAMES NAPIER

- ly place ___ at the best ___ of times, ___ Lord ___
- got fast; ___ good ___ things ___ don't last ___ an - y
- er know ___ all the beau - ti - ful things we could

knows. _
more. __
be. ____

1
I won't lie ___

2
Now _

___ and then ___ you cross ___ my mind. _ It takes ___ me back ___ to a sweet-

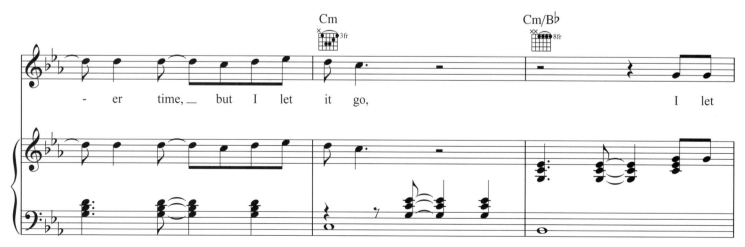

- er time, __ but I let it go, I let

Now my heart ___ is bro - ken and I'm cry - ing on the floor, ___ and ev -

'ry part of me ___ hopes you walk ___ through the door. ___ But you're not ___

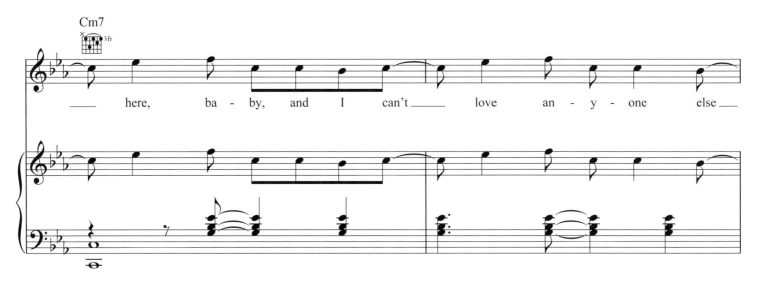

___ here, ba - by, and I can't ___ love an - y - one else ___

___ till I ___ for - give ___ my - self. ___

LOVE GOES

Words and Music by SAM SMITH
and TIMOTHY LEE McKENZIE

Very freely

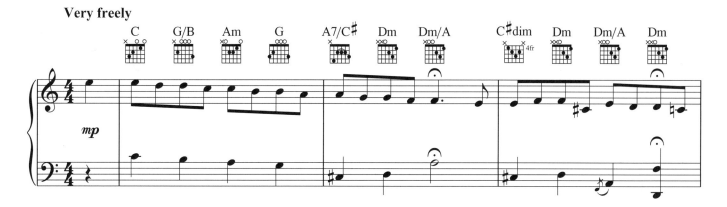

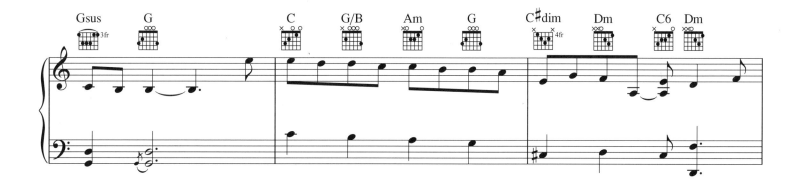

Moderately slow, expressively

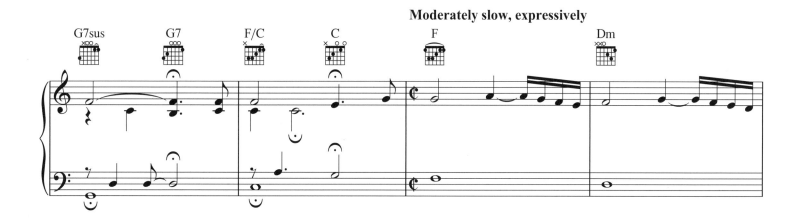

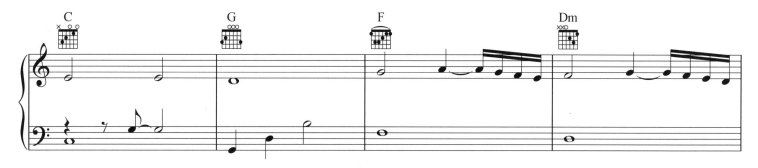

Moderately, in 2

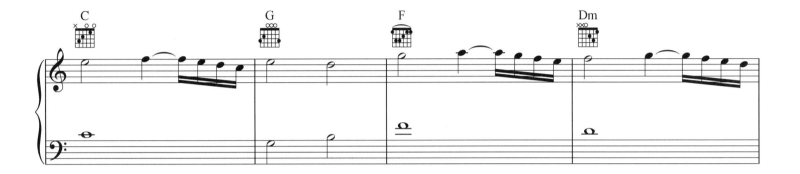

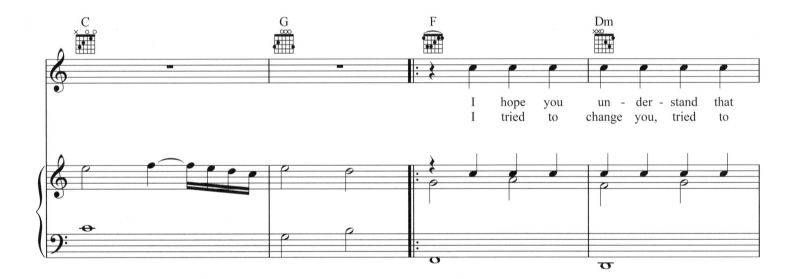

I hope you un-der-stand that
I tried to change you, tried to

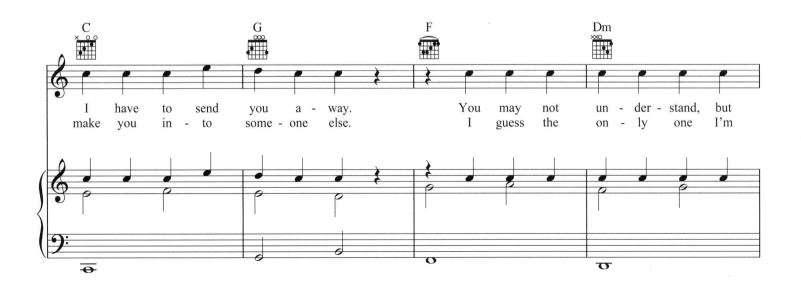

I have to send you a-way.
make you in-to some-one else.

You may not un-der-stand, but
I guess the on-ly one I'm

goes, _____ that's how love goes. __
goes, _____ that's how love goes, __

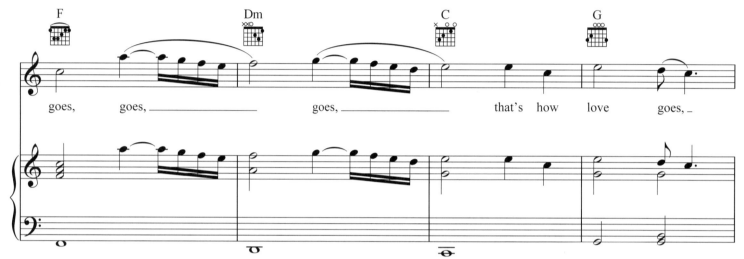

goes, goes, _____ goes, _____ that's how love goes, _

To Coda ⊕

goes, goes, _____ goes, _____ that's how love... Say

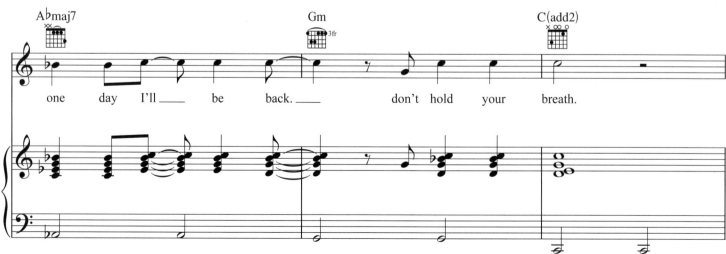

one day I'll __ be back. __ don't hold your breath.

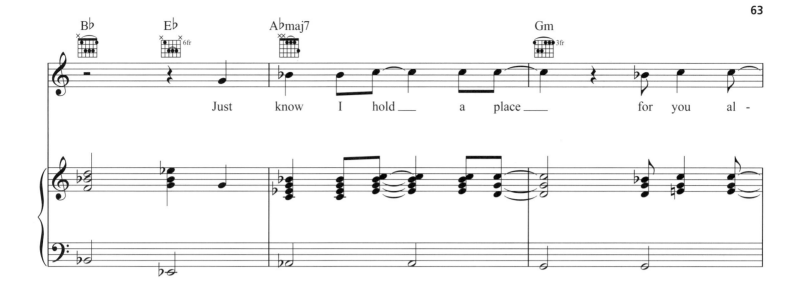

Just know I hold ___ a place ___ for you al-

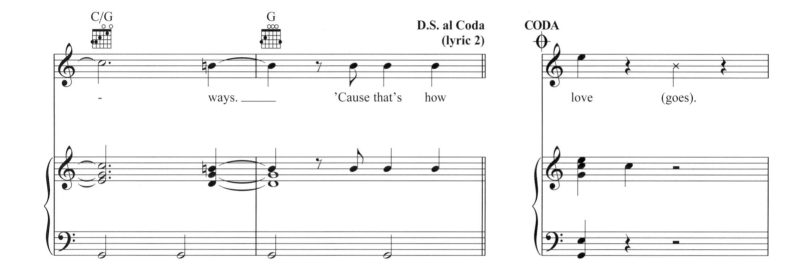

-ways. ___ 'Cause that's how

love (goes).

D.S. al Coda
(lyric 2)

CODA

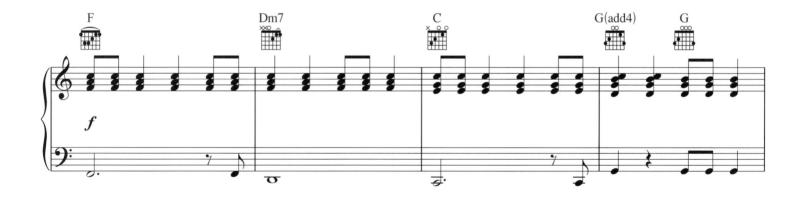

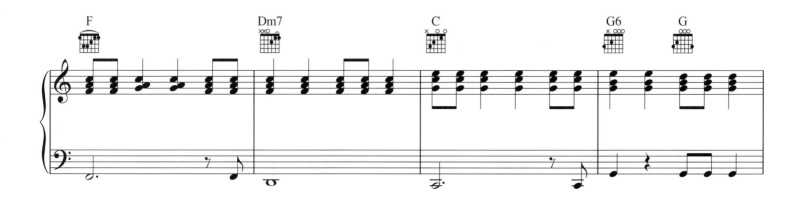

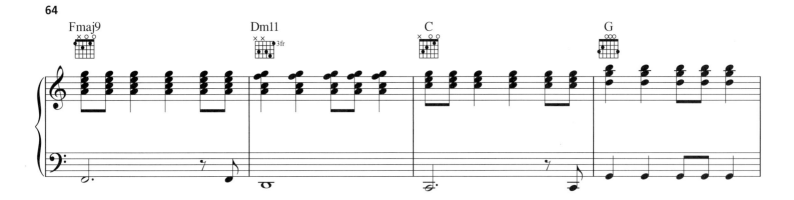

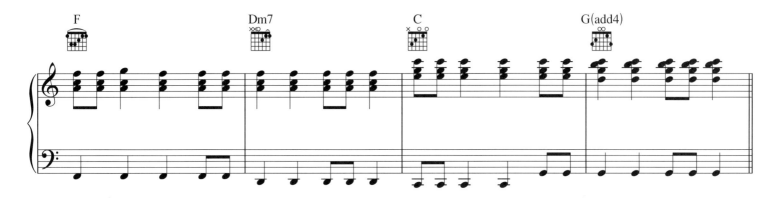

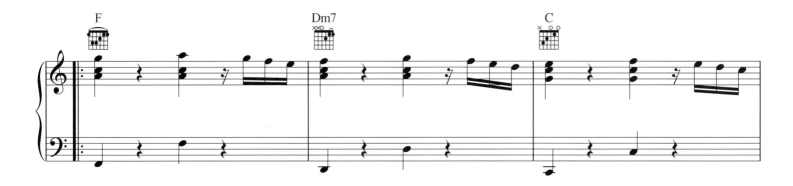

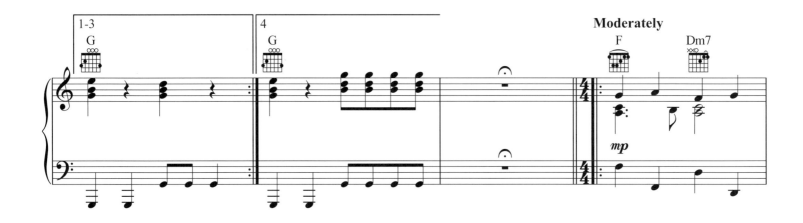

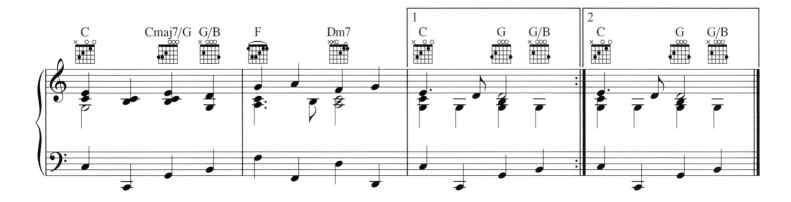

KIDS AGAIN

Words and Music by SAM SMITH,
LOUIS BELL, ALEXANDRA TAMPOSI,
ANDREW WOTMAN and RYAN TEDDER

Moderately slow

Can't be-lieve I still a-void the east side, e - ven though I know that you don't live there now.
Liv-ing out of suit-cas-es and ho - tels, drink-ing way too much and talk-ing through the night.

Late-ly you're the on - ly thing on my mind. And I can't stop my-self from driv-ing by your house.
Real-ly wish I did-n't know you so well. Would-n't be so hard to leave the past be - hind.

Ooh, ev - 'ry time I hear our song, it kind of hurts me still. And, ___

* Recorded a half step lower. Guitar is tuned down a half step.

ooh, e - ven af - ter all this time, I kind - a miss you still. I'm won - der - ing:

Do you e - ven think a - bout __ it? __ The way that we changed __ the world. __ And don't it

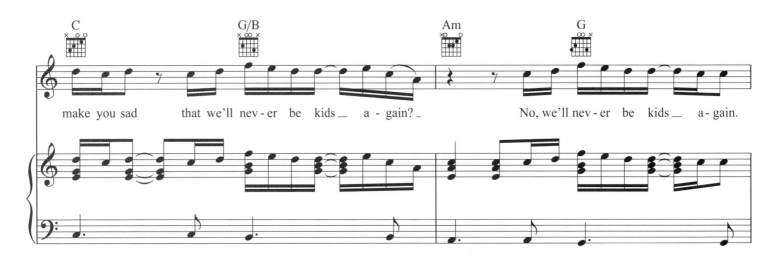

make you sad that we'll nev - er be kids __ a - gain? __ No, we'll nev - er be kids __ a - gain.

Tell me how you live with - out __ it. __ Did some - bod - y change __ your world __ and now you

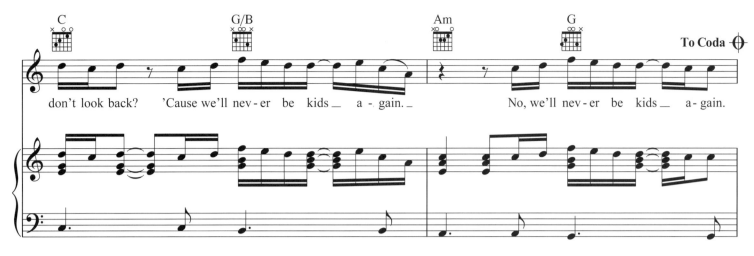

To Coda ⊕

don't look back? 'Cause we'll nev - er be kids __ a - gain. __ No, we'll nev - er be kids __ a - gain.

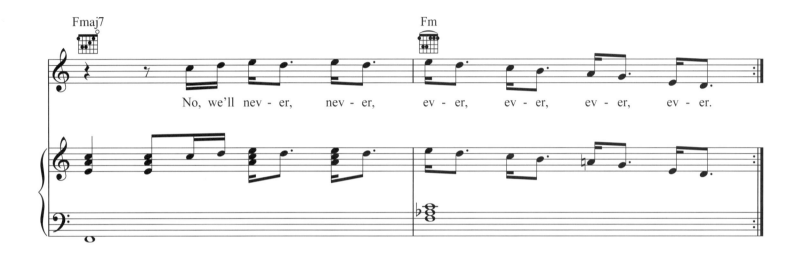

No, we'll nev - er, nev - er, ev - er, ev - er, ev - er, ev - er.

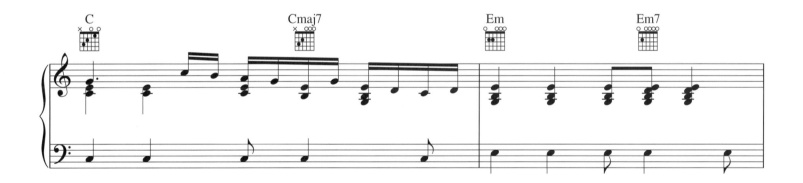

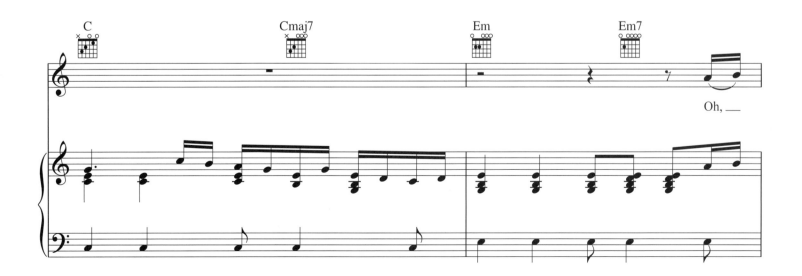

Oh, __

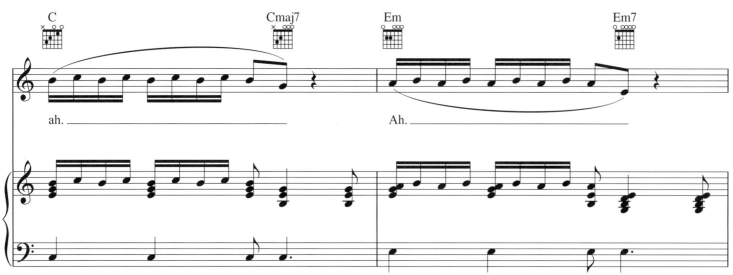

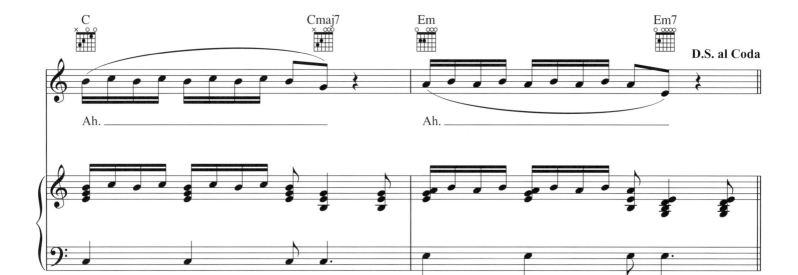

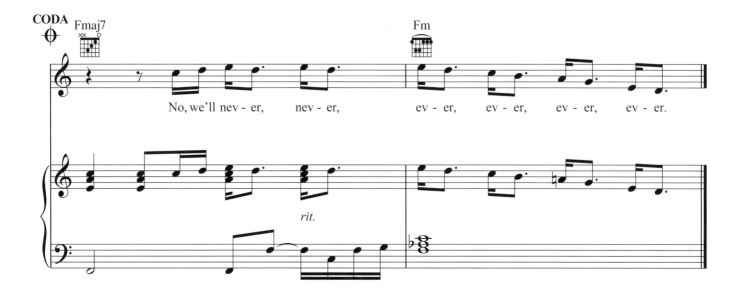

DANCING WITH A STRANGER

Words and Music by SAM SMITH,
TOR HERMANSEN, MIKKEL ERIKSEN,
NORMANI HAMILTON and JAMES NAPIER

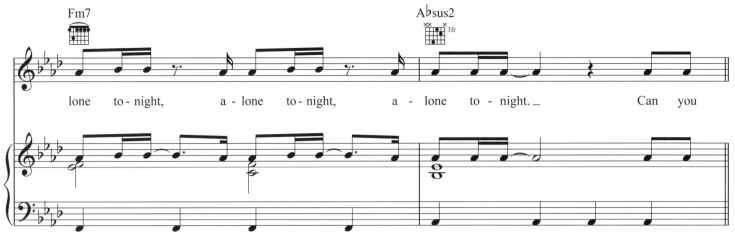

lone to-night, a - lone to-night, a - lone to-night. __ Can you

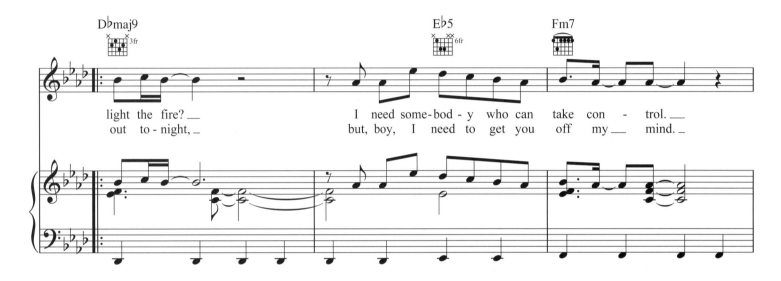

light the fire? __ I need some-bod - y who can take con - trol. __
out to-night, __ but, boy, I need to get you off my __ mind. __

I know ex - act - ly what I need to __ do, __ 'cause I don't wan - na be a -
I know ex - act - ly what I have to __ do. __ I don't wan - na be a -

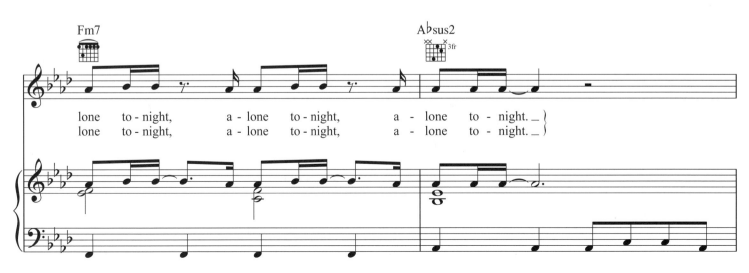

lone to-night, a - lone to-night, a - lone to-night. __ }
lone to-night, a - lone to-night, a - lone to-night. __ }

* Female vocal sung one octave lower.

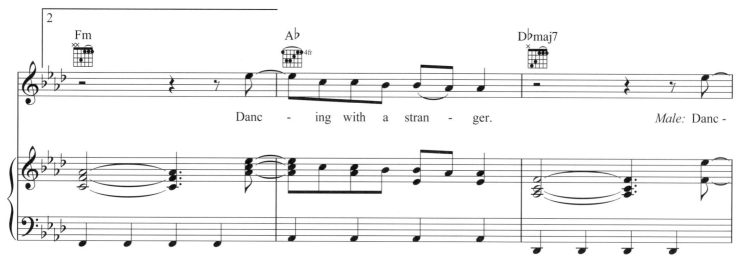

Danc - - ing with a stran - ger. *Male:* Danc -

- ing, yeah, — yeah.

Look what you made me do; I'm with some-bod - y new. Ooh, ba - by, ba - by, I'm danc -

- ing with a stran - ger. *Both:* Look what you made me do; I'm with some-bod - y new.

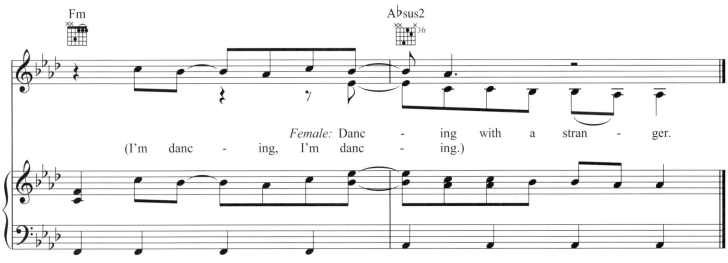

Female vocal written at sung pitch (bottom notes).

HOW DO YOU SLEEP?

Words and Music by SAM SMITH,
MAX MARTIN, SAVAN KOTECHA
and ILYA SALMANZADEH

Pop Ballad

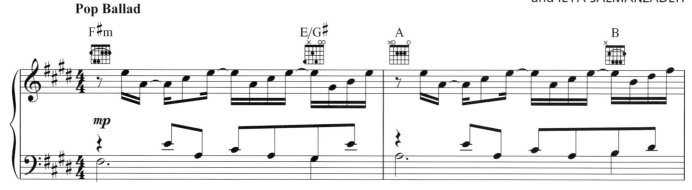

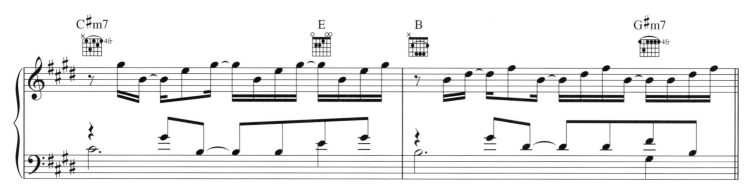

I'm __ done hat-ing my-self for feel — ing.

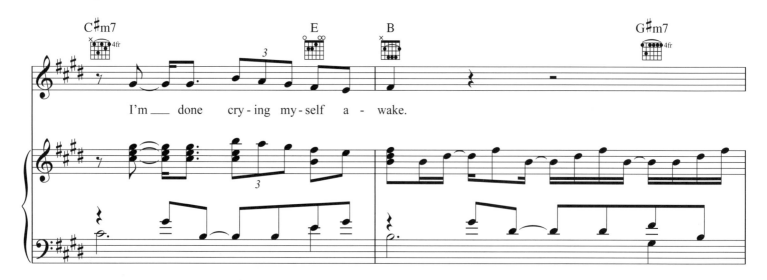

I'm __ done cry-ing my-self a - wake.

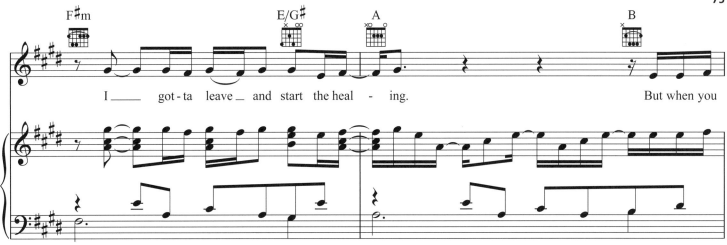

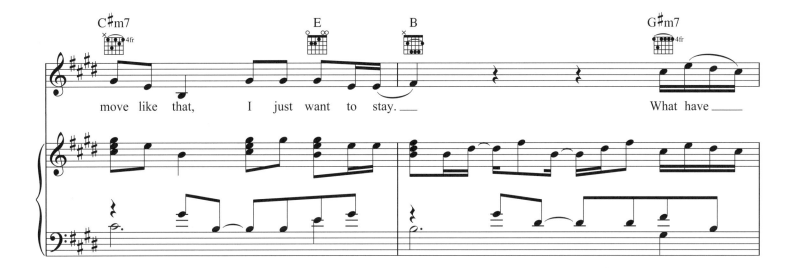

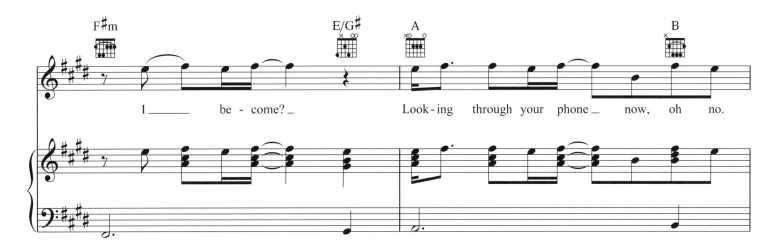

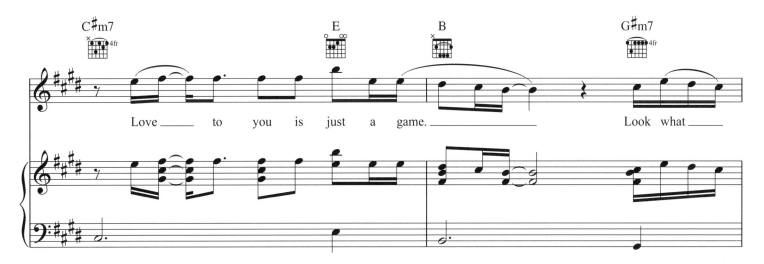

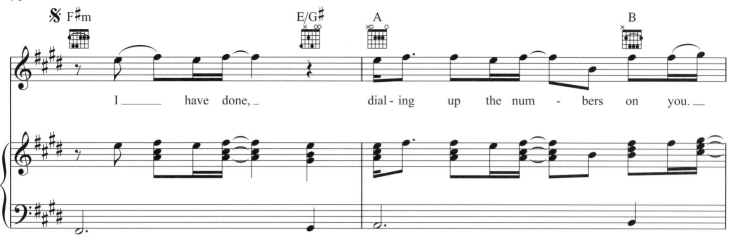

I ___ have done, _ dial - ing up the num - bers on you. ___

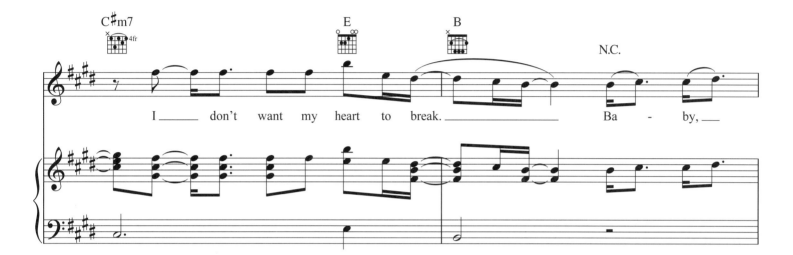

I ___ don't want my heart to break. _____ Ba - by, ___

how do you sleep when you lie to me? _ All that shame and all ___ that dan - ger.

I'm hop - ing that my love will keep you up ___ to - night. Ba - by,

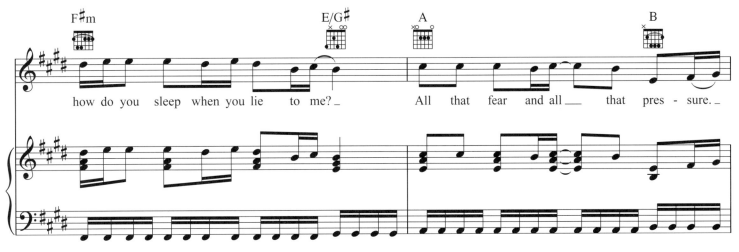

how do you sleep when you lie to me? _ All that fear and all __ that pres - sure. _

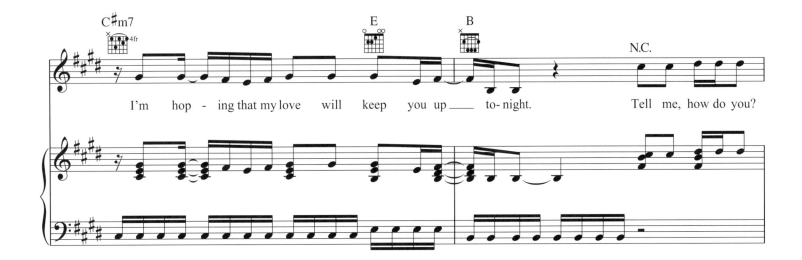

I'm hop - ing that my love will keep you up __ to- night. Tell me, how do you?

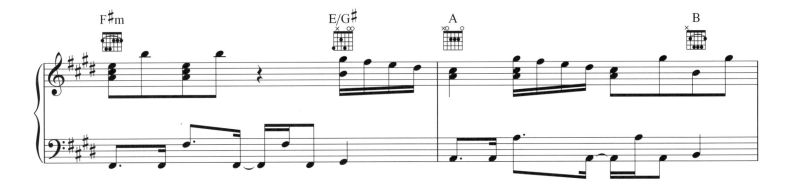

To Coda ⊕

Love _ will _ keep you up to - night. Tell me, how do you?

up to-night. _ Tell me, how do you?

Love _ will _ keep you up to-night. _ Ba - by,

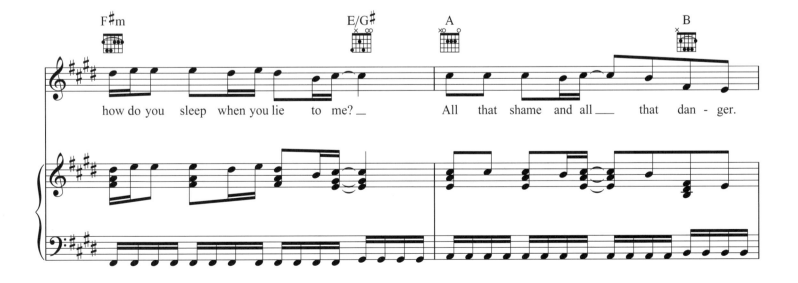

how do you sleep when you lie to me? _ All that shame and all _ that dan - ger.

I'm hop - ing that my love will keep you up ____ to - night. Ba - by,

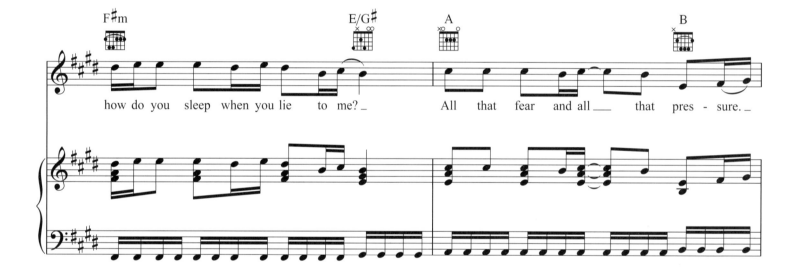

how do you sleep when you lie to me? _ All that fear and all ___ that pres - sure. _

I'm hop - ing that my love will keep you up ____ to - night. Tell me, how do you?

TO DIE FOR

Words and Music by SAM SMITH,
TOR HERMANSEN, MIKKEL ERIKSEN
and JAMES NAPIER

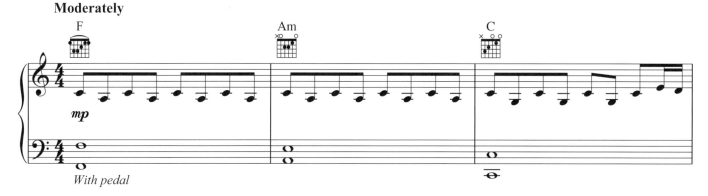

I ___ look for you ___ ev-'ry

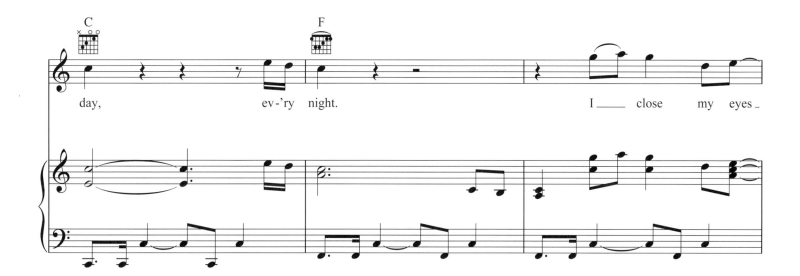

day, ev-'ry night. I ___ close my eyes_

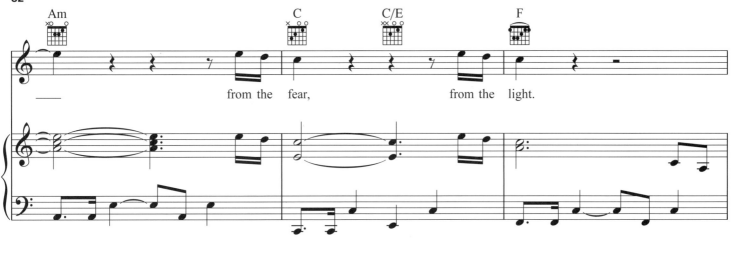

from the fear, from the light.

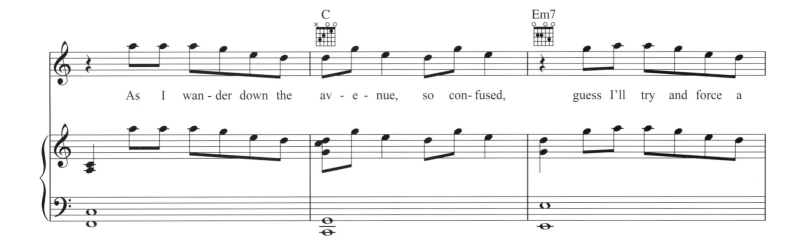

As I wan-der down the av-e-nue, so con-fused, guess I'll try and force a

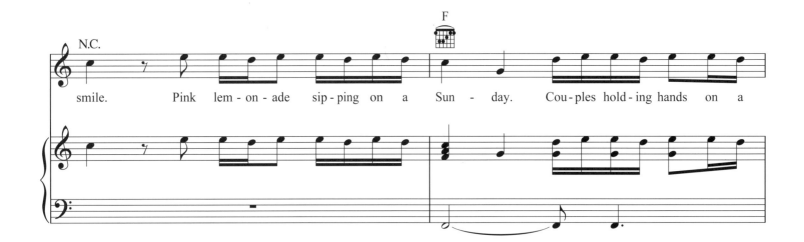

smile. Pink lem-on-ade sip-ping on a Sun - day. Cou-ples hold-ing hands on a

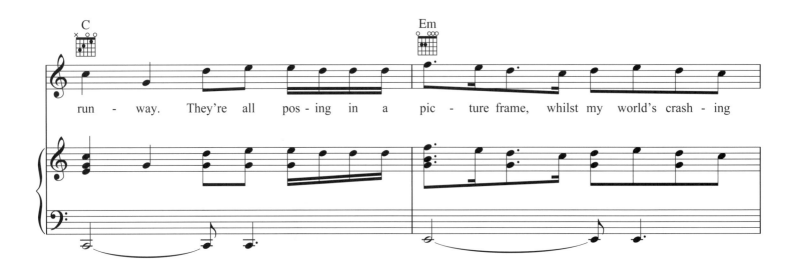

run - way. They're all pos-ing in a pic - ture frame, whilst my world's crash-ing

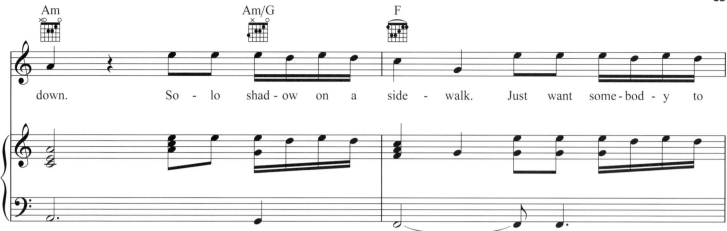

down. So - lo shad - ow on a side - walk. Just want some - bod - y to

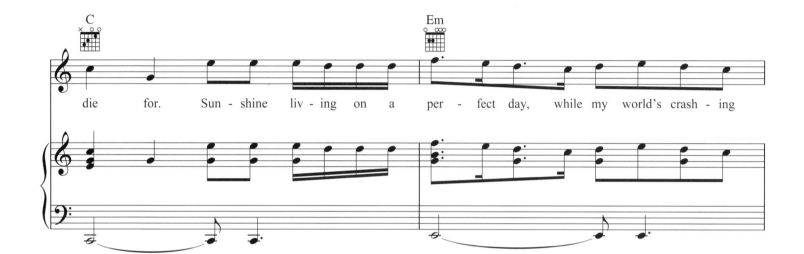

die for. Sun - shine liv - ing on a per - fect day, while my world's crash - ing

down. I just want some - bod - y to die ___ for.

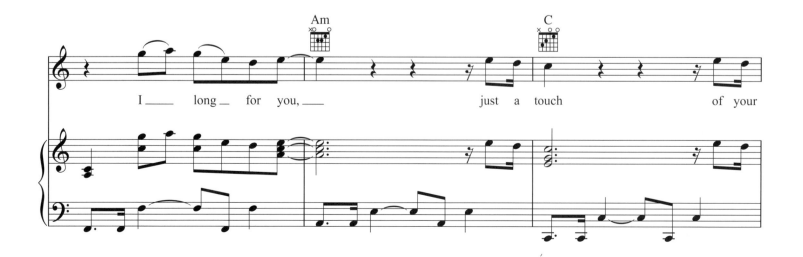

I ___ long ___ for you, ___ just a touch of your

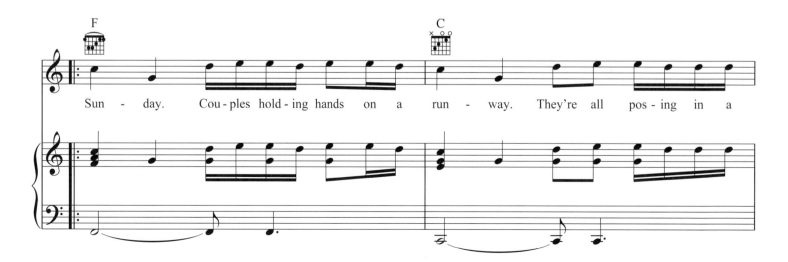

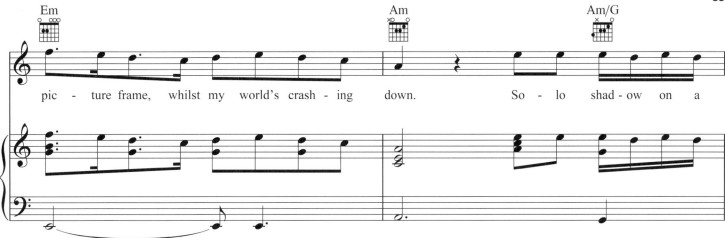

pic - ture frame, whilst my world's crash - ing down. So - lo shad - ow on a

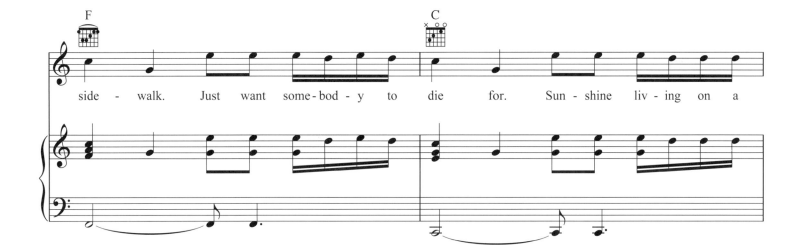

side - walk. Just want some-bod - y to die for. Sun - shine liv - ing on a

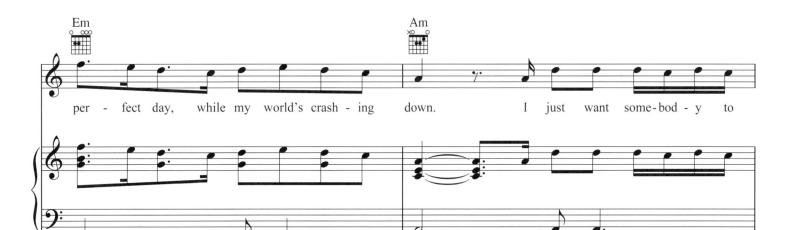

per - fect day, while my world's crash - ing down. I just want some-bod - y to

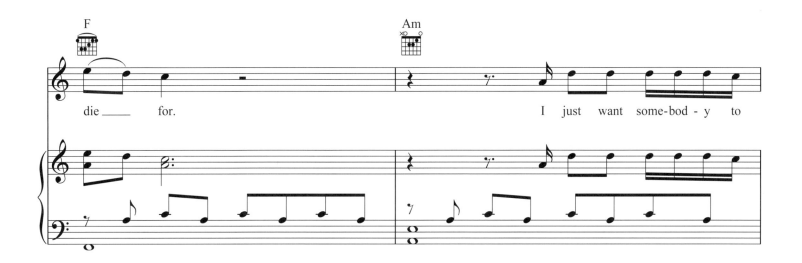

die ___ for. I just want some-bod - y to

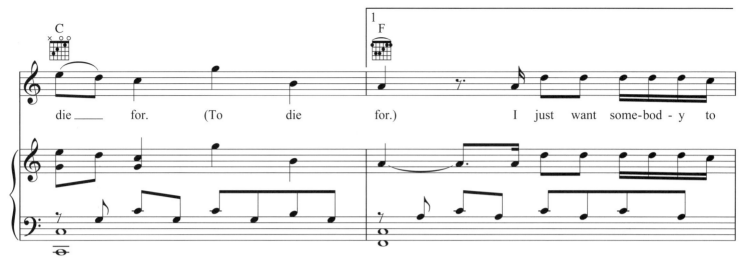

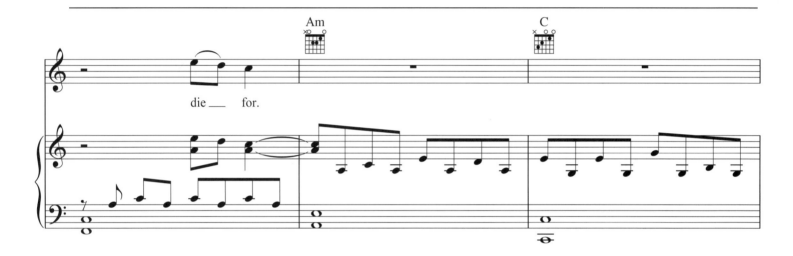

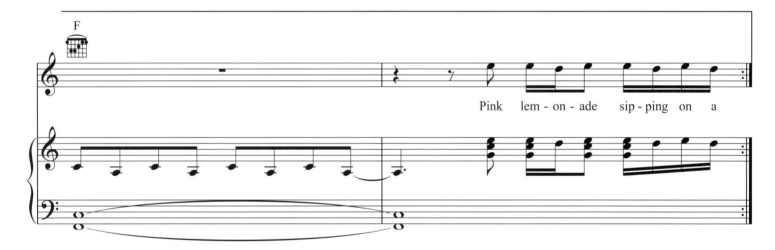

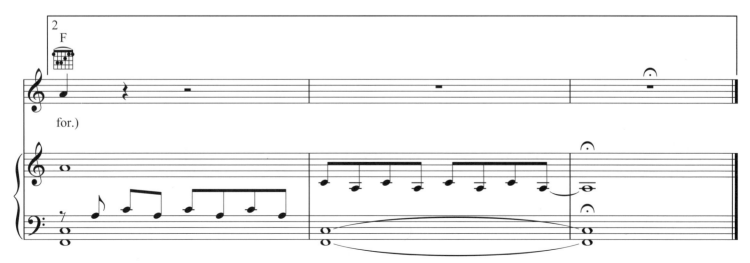

I'M READY

Words and Music by SAM SMITH,
DEMITRIA LOVATO, SAVAN KOTECHA,
ANDERS PETER SVENSSON and ILYA SALMANZADEH

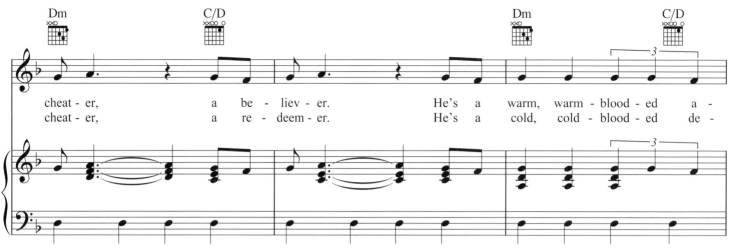

cheat - er, a be - liev - er. He's a warm, warm - blood - ed a -
cheat - er, a re - deem - er. He's a cold, cold - blood - ed de -

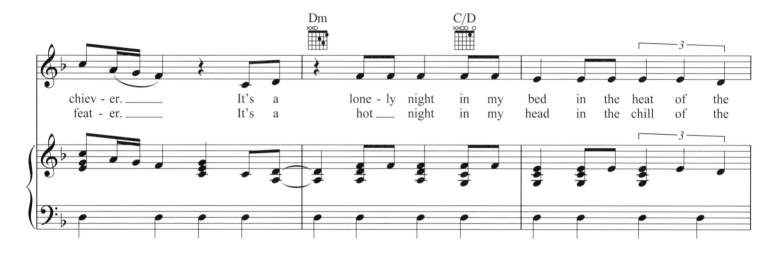

chiev - er. _____ It's a lone - ly night in my bed in the heat of the
feat - er. _____ It's a hot ___ night in my head in the chill of the

sum - mer. Oh. _____ } *Male:* It's so hard _____ when you're
win - ter, no. _____ }

with some - one, your heart _____ breaks and it ain't no fun. But

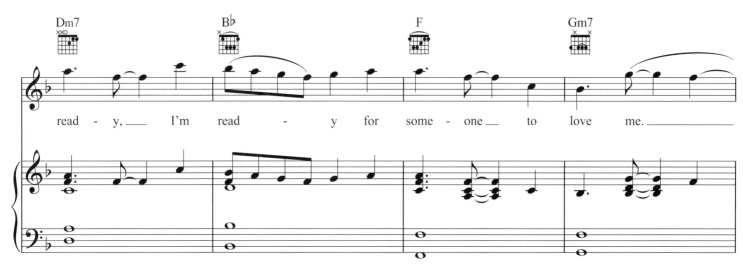

* Female sings 2nd time 8vb.

read - y, ___ I'm read - y for some - one ___ to

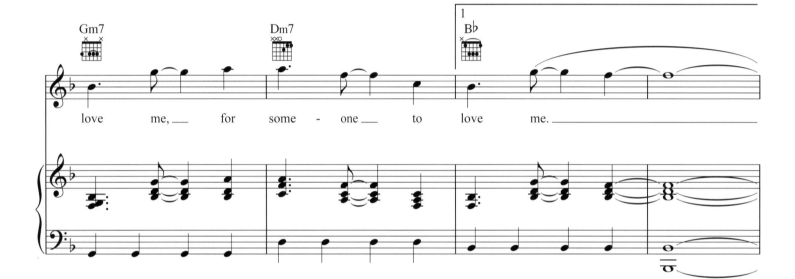

love me, ___ for some - one ___ to love me. ___

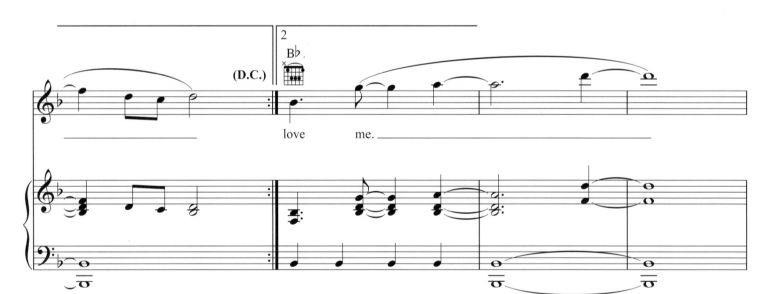

(D.C.) love me. ___

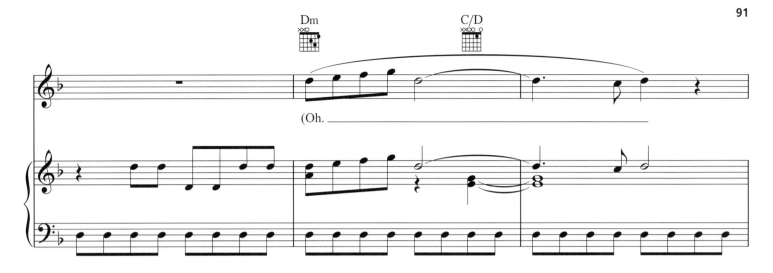

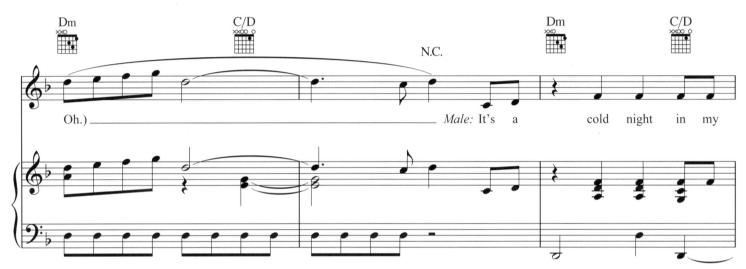

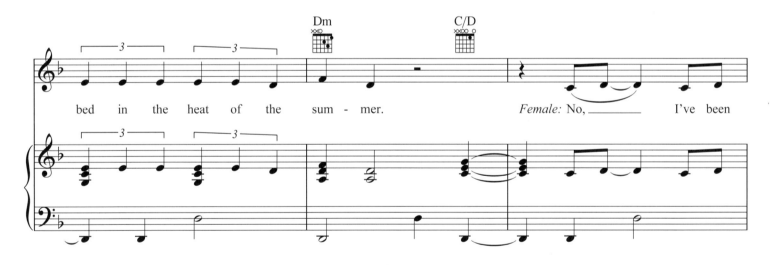

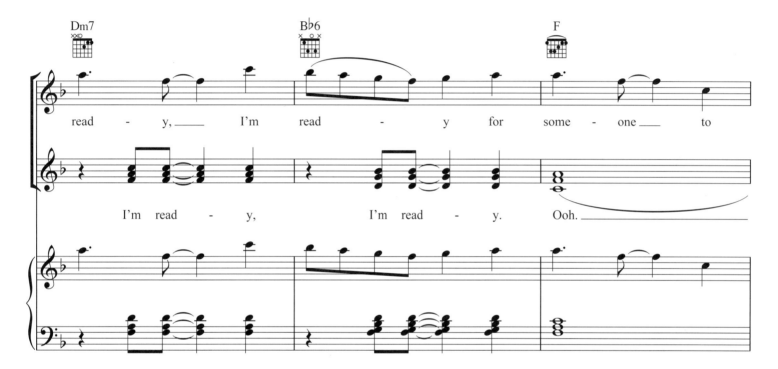

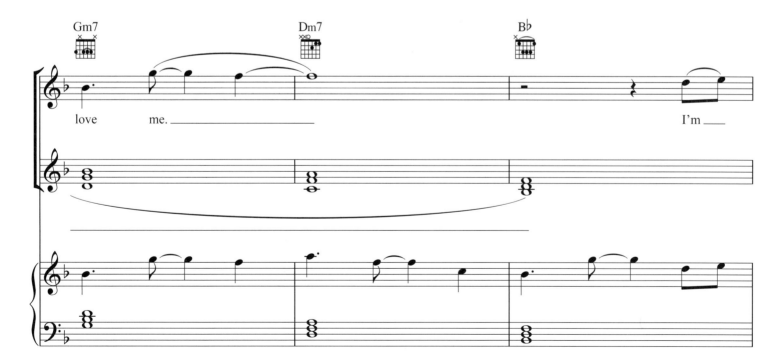

read - y, ___ I'm read - y, ___ I'm read - y, ___ I'm

I'm read - y, I'm read - y, I'm read - y,

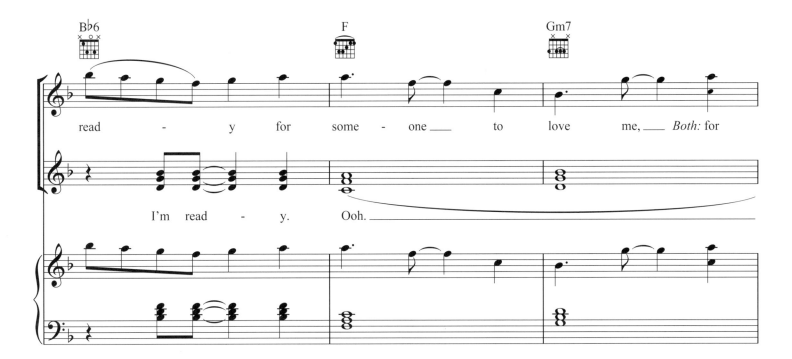

read - y for some - one ___ to love me, ___ *Both:* for

I'm read - y. Ooh. ___

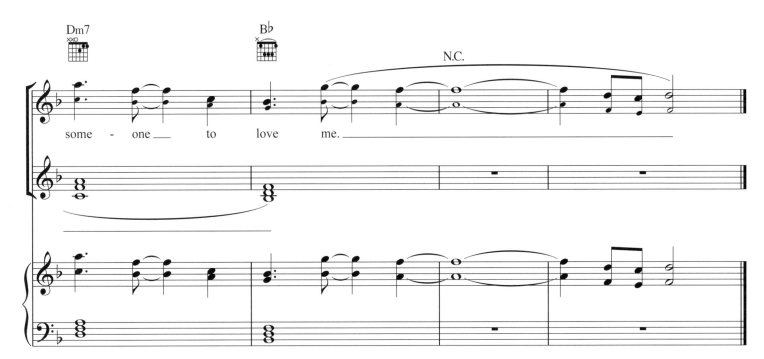

some - one ___ to love me. ___

FIRE ON FIRE

Words and Music by SAM SMITH
and STEVE MAC

Moderately fast

My moth-er said I'm too ro-man-tic.

She said, "You're danc-ing in the mov-ies." I al-most start-ed to be-

lieve her, then I saw you and I knew.

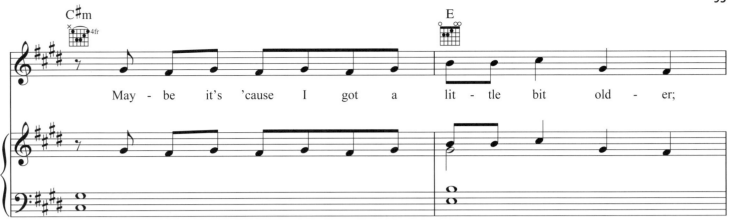

May-be it's 'cause I got a lit-tle bit old -er;

may-be it's all that I've been through. I'd like to think it's how you

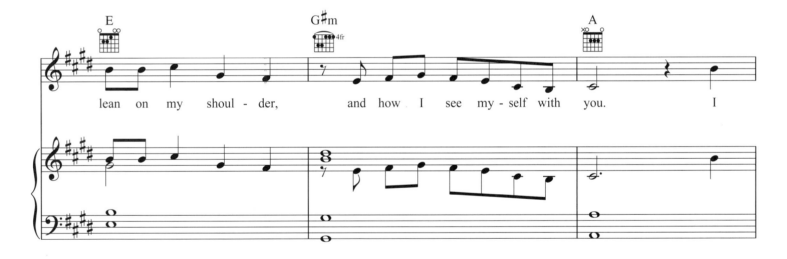

lean on my shoul -der, and how I see my-self with you. I

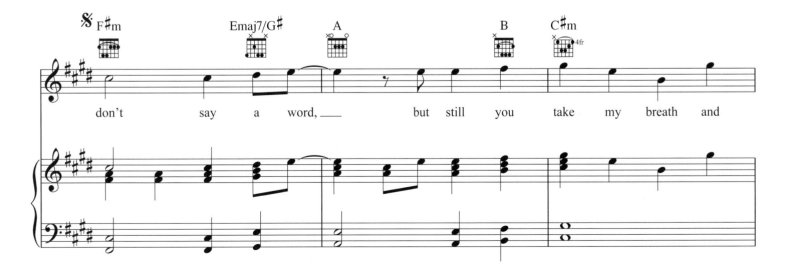

don't say a word, ___ but still you take my breath and

steal the things I know. ___ There you go, ___ sav - ing

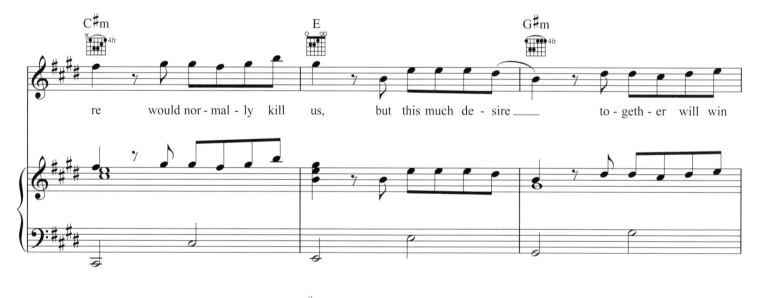

me from out of the cold. Fi - re on fi -

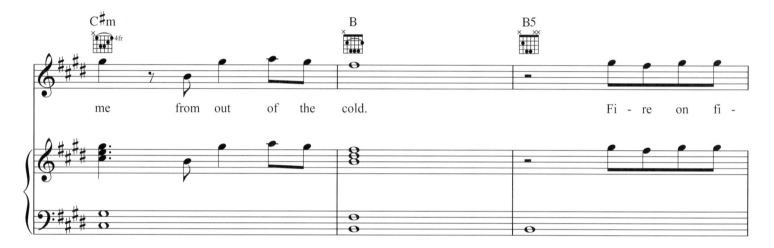

re would nor - mal - ly kill us, but this much de - sire ___ to - geth - er will win

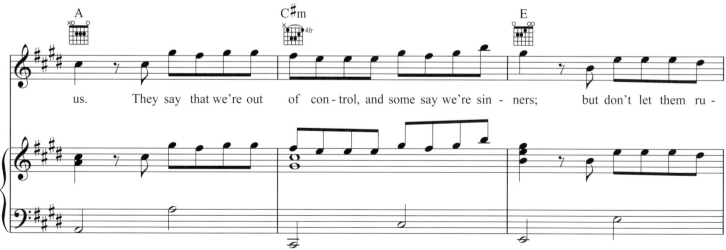

us. They say that we're out of con - trol, and some say we're sin - ners; but don't let them ru -

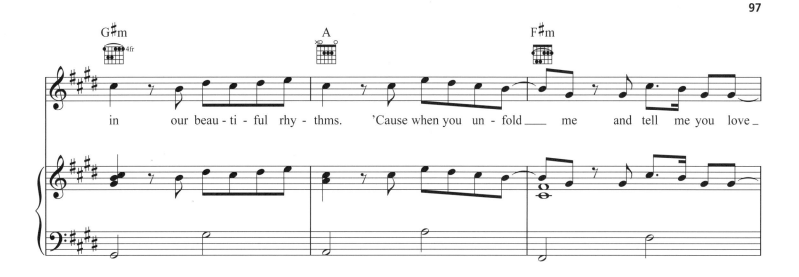

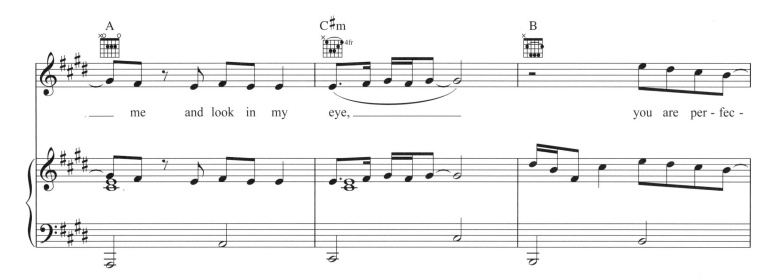

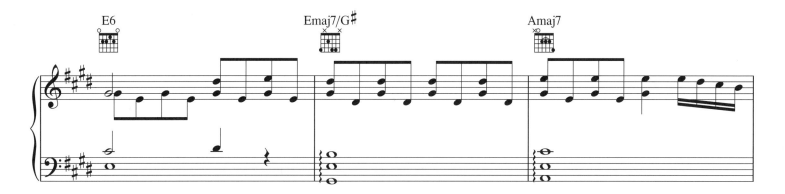

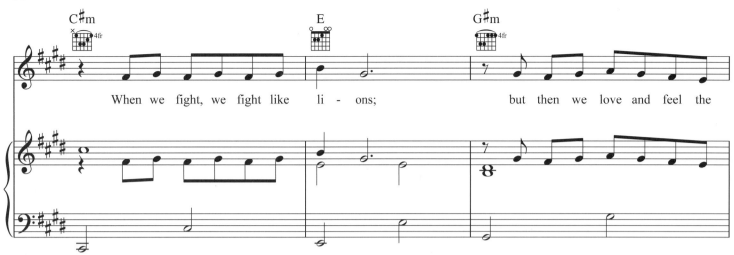

When we fight, we fight like li - ons; but then we love and feel the

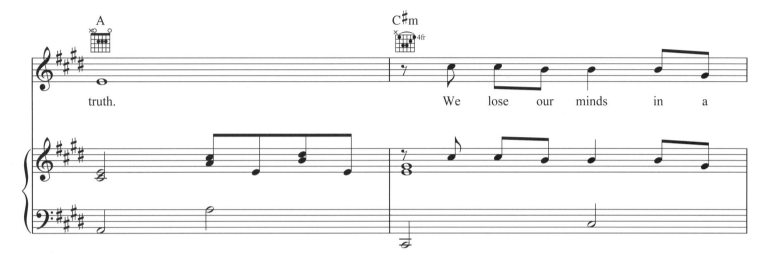

truth. We lose our minds in a

cit - y of ros - es; we won't a - bide by an - y rules. I

D.S. al Coda

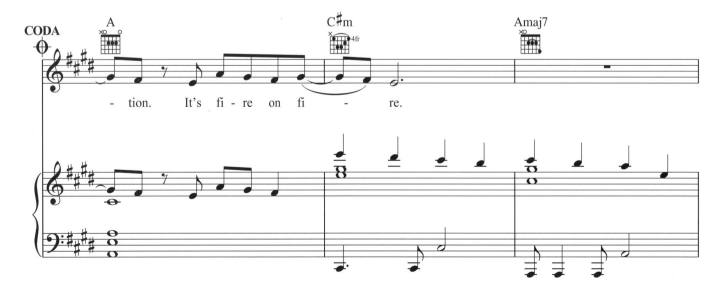

CODA

- tion. It's fi - re on fi - re.

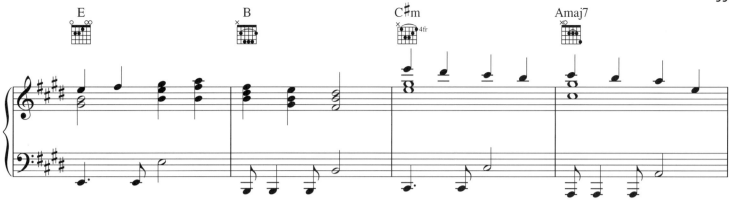

Fi - re on fi - re would nor - mal - ly kill

us, but this much de - sire _____ to - geth - er will win us. They say that we're out

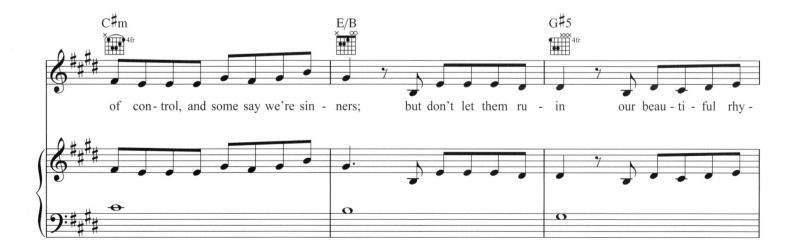

of con - trol, and some say we're sin - ners; but don't let them ru - in our beau - ti - ful rhy -

thms. Fi - re on fi - re would nor - mal - ly kill us, but this much de - sire __

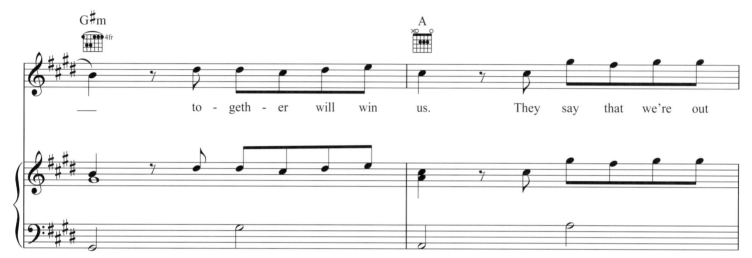

__ to - geth - er will win us. They say that we're out

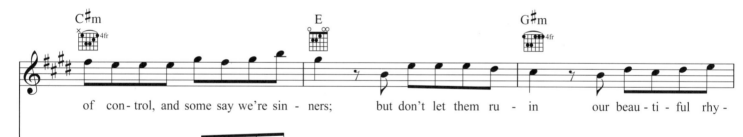

of con - trol, and some say we're sin - ners; but don't let them ru - in our beau - ti - ful rhy-

thms. 'Cause when you un - fold __ me and tell me you love __ me and look in my eyes, __

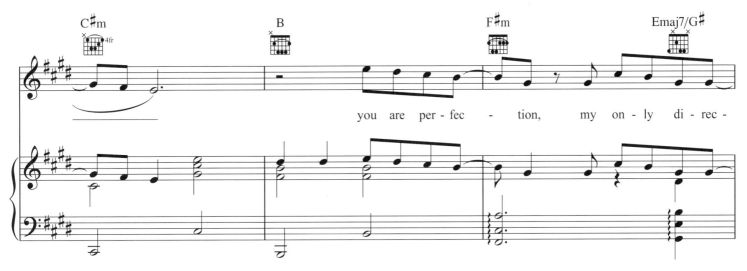

you are per - fec - tion, my on - ly di - rec -

- tion. It's fi - re on fire. _____ You are per - fec -

- tion, my on - ly di - rec - tion. _ It's fi - re on fire. _____

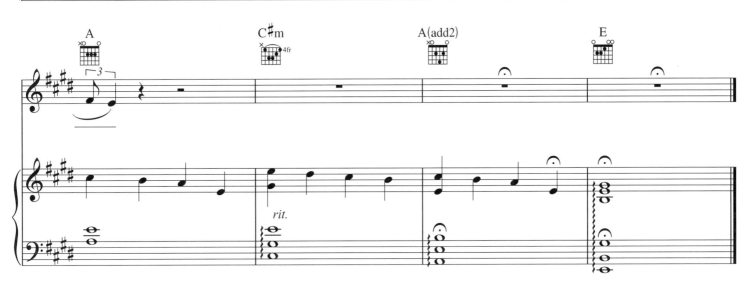

PROMISES

Words and Music by CALVIN HARRIS,
SAM SMITH and JESSICA REYES

* *Recorded a half step lower.*

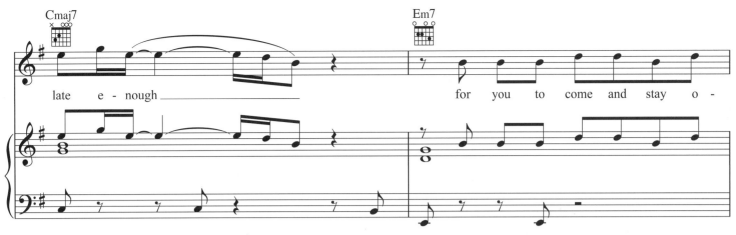

late e - nough _____ for you to come and stay o -

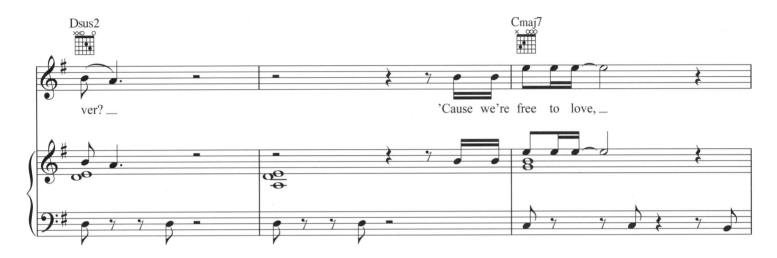

ver? _ 'Cause we're free to love, _

so tease me, hmm. _____

I make no prom-is - es, _ I can't do gold-en rings but I'll give you ev -'ry-thing _ (to -

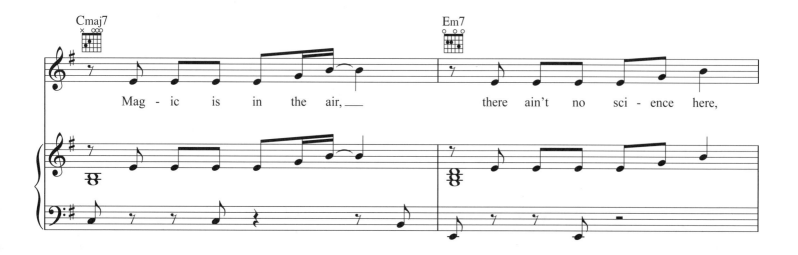

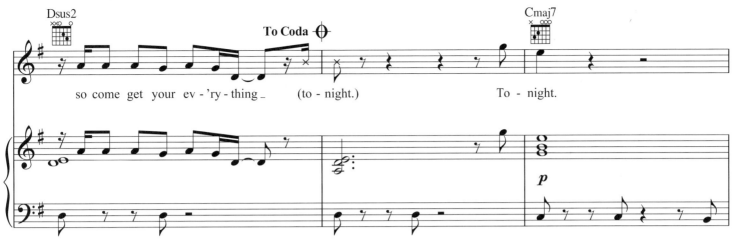

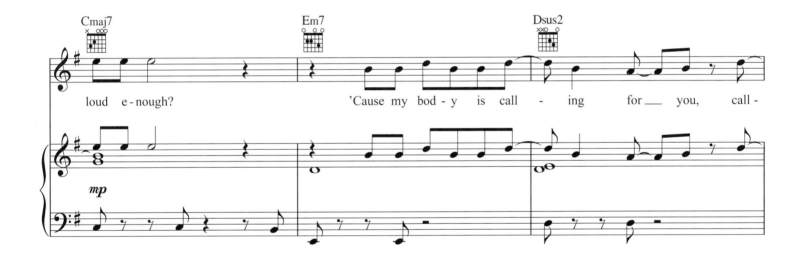

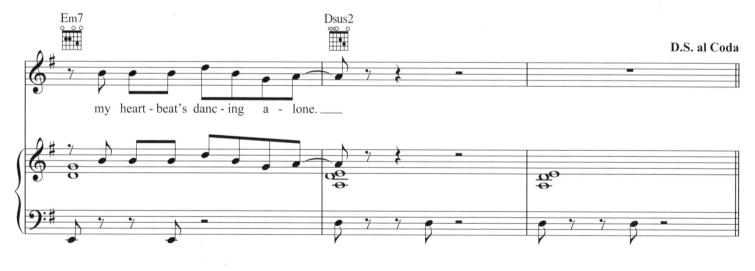

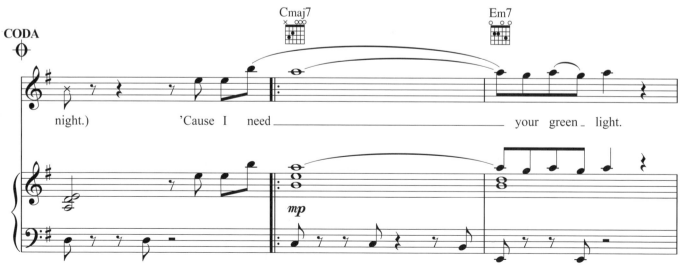

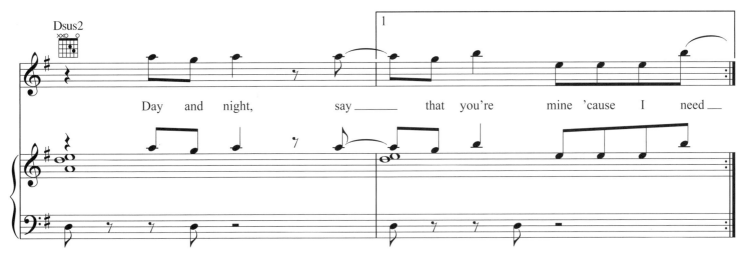

Day and night, say ___ that you're mine 'cause I need ___

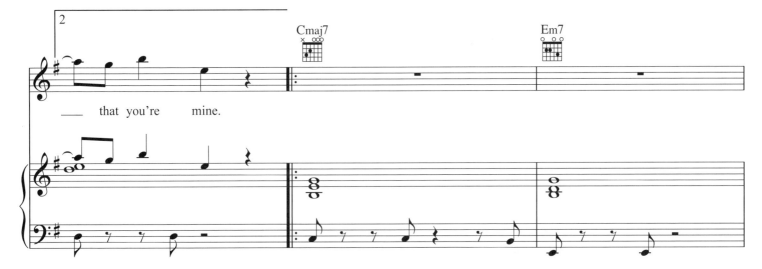

___ that you're mine.

Say ___ that you're mine. ___ that you're mine.

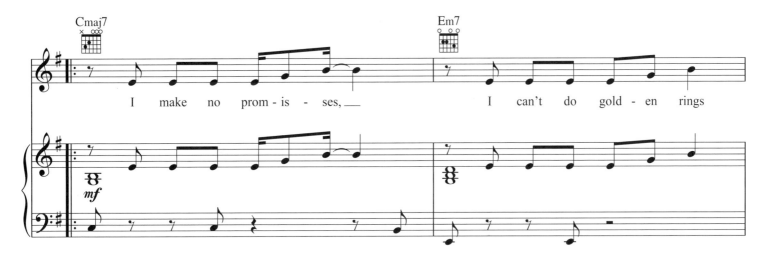

I make no prom-is-ses, ___ I can't do gold-en rings

but I'll give you ev - 'ry - thing __ (to - night.)

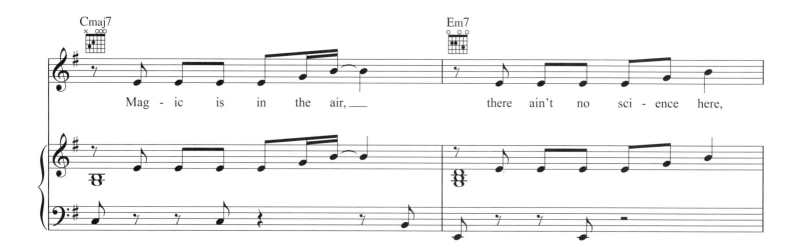

Mag - ic is in the air, __ there ain't no sci - ence here,

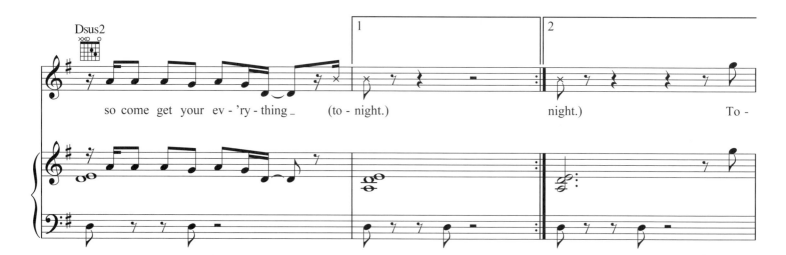

so come get your ev - 'ry - thing __ (to - night.)   night.)   To -

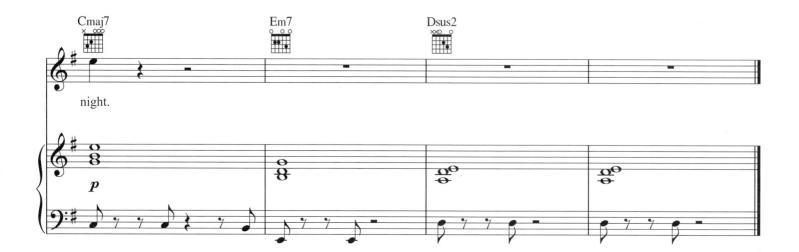

night.

More Songbooks from Your Favorite Artists

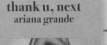

ADELE – 25

22 songs: All I Ask • Hello – I Miss You • Million Years Ago • River Lea • Send My Love (To Your New Lover) • Water Under the Bridge • When We Were Young • and more.

00155393 Piano/Vocal/Guitar $19.99

SARA BAREILLES – AMIDST THE CHAOS

12 songs: Armor • Fire • No Such Thing • Poetry by Dead Men • A Safe Place to Land (feat. John Legend) • Saint Honesty • and more.

00294277 Piano/Vocal/Guitar $19.99

LEWIS CAPALDI – DIVINELY UNINSPIRED TO A HELLISH EXTENT

Bruises • Don't Get Me Wrong • Fade • Forever • Grace • Headspace • Hold Me While You Wait • Hollywood • Lost on You • Maybe • One • Someone You Loved.

00299905 Piano/Vocal/Guitar $19.99

COLDPLAY – EVERYDAY LIFE

16 tracks featuring the title track plus: Arabesque • Broken • Champion of the World • Church • Cry Cry Cry • Daddy • Eko • Guns • Sunrise • When I Need a Friend • and more.

00327962 Piano/Vocal/Guitar $19.99

BILLIE EILISH – WHEN WE ALL FALL ASLEEP, WHERE DO WE GO?

13 songs: All the Good Girls Go to Hell • Bad Guy • Bury a Friend • 8 • Goodbye • I Love You • ilomilo • Listen Before I Go • My Strange Addiction • When the Party's Over • Wish You Were Gay • Xanny • You Should See Me in a Crown.

00295684 Piano/Vocal/Guitar $19.99

ARIANA GRANDE – THANK U, NEXT

11 songs: Bad Idea • Bloodline • Break up with Your Girlfriend, I'm Bored • Fake Smile • Ghostin • Imagine • In My Head • Make Up • NASA • Needy • 7 Rings.

00292769 Piano/Vocal/Guitar $19.99

LIZZO – CUZ I LOVE YOU

12 songs: Better in Color • Crybaby • Cuz I Love You • Exactly How I Feel • Heaven Help Me • Jerome • Juice • Like a Girl • Lingerie • Soulmate • Tempo • Truth Hurts.

00304758 Piano/Vocal/Guitar $19.99

THE LUMINEERS – III

13 songs: April • Democracy • Donna • Gloria • It Wasn't Easy to Be Happy for You • Jimmy Sparks • Leader of the Landslide • Left for Denver • Life in the City • My Cell • Old Lady • Salt and the Sea • Soundtrack Song.

00322983 Piano/Vocal/Guitar $19.99

SHAWN MENDES

14 songs: Because I Had You • Fallin' All in You • In My Blood • Like to Be You • Lost in Japan • Mutual • Nervous • Particular Taste • Perfectly Wrong • Queen • When You're Ready, I'm Waiting • Where Were You in the Morning? • Why • Youth.

00279536 Piano/Vocal/Guitar $17.99

HARRY STYLES – FINE LINE

12 songs: Adore You • Canyon Moon • Cherry • Falling • Fine Line • Golden • Lights Up • She • Sunflower, Vol. 6 • To Be So Lonely • Treat People with Kindness • Watermelon Sugar.

00338558 Piano/Vocal/Guitar $19.99

TAYLOR SWIFT – FOLKLORE

17 songs: Betty • Cardigan • Exile (feat. Bon Iver) • Illicit Affairs • The Lakes • The Last Great American Dynasty • Mad Woman • The 1 • Peace • and more.

00356804 Piano/Vocal/Guitar $19.99

For a complete listing of the products available, visit us online at **www.halleonard.com**

Contents, prices, and availability subject to change without notice.

0920
015

THE NEW DECADE SERIES

 Books with Online Audio • Arranged for Piano, Voice, and Guitar

The New Decade Series features collections of iconic songs from each decade with great backing tracks so you can play them and sound like a pro. You access the tracks online for streaming or download. **See complete song listings online at www.halleonard.com**

SONGS OF THE 1920s
Ain't Misbehavin' • Baby Face • California, Here I Come • Fascinating Rhythm • I Wanna Be Loved by You • It Had to Be You • Mack the Knife • Ol' Man River • Puttin' on the Ritz • Rhapsody in Blue • Someone to Watch over Me • Tea for Two • Who's Sorry Now • and more.
00137576 P/V/G....................................$27.99

SONGS OF THE 1930s
As Time Goes By • Blue Moon • Cheek to Cheek • Embraceable You • A Fine Romance • Georgia on My Mind • I Only Have Eyes for You • The Lady Is a Tramp • On the Sunny Side of the Street • Over the Rainbow • Pennies from Heaven • Stormy Weather (Keeps Rainin' All the Time) • The Way You Look Tonight • and more.
00137579 P/V/G....................................$24.99

SONGS OF THE 1940s
At Last • Boogie Woogie Bugle Boy • Don't Get Around Much Anymore • God Bless' the Child • How High the Moon • It Could Happen to You • La Vie En Rose (Take Me to Your Heart Again) • Route 66 • Sentimental Journey • The Trolley Song • You'd Be So Nice to Come Home To • Zip-A-Dee-Doo-Dah • and more.
00137582 P/V/G....................................$27.99

SONGS OF THE 1950s
Ain't That a Shame • Be-Bop-A-Lula • Chantilly Lace • Earth Angel • Fever • Great Balls of Fire • Love Me Tender • Mona Lisa • Peggy Sue • Que Sera, Sera (Whatever Will Be, Will Be) • Rock Around the Clock • Sixteen Tons • A Teenager in Love • That'll Be the Day • Unchained Melody • Volare • You Send Me • Your Cheatin' Heart • and more.
00137595 P/V/G....................................$24.99

SONGS OF THE 1960s
All You Need Is Love • Beyond the Sea • Born to Be Wild • California Girls • Dancing in the Street • Happy Together • King of the Road • Leaving on a Jet Plane • Louie, Louie • My Generation • Oh, Pretty Woman • Sunshine of Your Love • Under the Boardwalk • You Really Got Me • and more.
00137596 P/V/G....................................$27.99

SONGS OF THE 1970s
ABC • Bridge over Troubled Water • Cat's in the Cradle • Dancing Queen • Free Bird • Goodbye Yellow Brick Road • Hotel California • I Will Survive • Joy to the World • Killing Me Softly with His Song • Layla • Let It Be • Piano Man • The Rainbow Connection • Stairway to Heaven • The Way We Were • Your Song • and more.
00137599 P/V/G....................................$29.99

SONGS OF THE 1980s
Addicted to Love • Beat It • Careless Whisper • Come on Eileen • Don't Stop Believin' • Every Rose Has Its Thorn • Footloose • I Just Called to Say I Love You • Jessie's Girl • Livin' on a Prayer • Saving All My Love for You • Take on Me • Up Where We Belong • The Wind Beneath My Wings • and more.
00137600 P/V/G....................................$29.99

SONGS OF THE 1990s
Angel • Black Velvet • Can You Feel the Love Tonight • (Everything I Do) I Do It for You • Friends in Low Places • Hero • I Will Always Love You • More Than Words • My Heart Will Go On (Love Theme from 'Titanic') • Smells like Teen Spirit • Under the Bridge • Vision of Love • Wonderwall • and more.
00137601 P/V/G....................................$27.99

SONGS OF THE 2000s
Bad Day • Beautiful • Before He Cheats • Chasing Cars • Chasing Pavements • Drops of Jupiter (Tell Me) • Fireflies • Hey There Delilah • How to Save a Life • I Gotta Feeling • I'm Yours • Just Dance • Love Story • 100 Years • Rehab • Unwritten • You Raise Me Up • and more.
00137608 P/V/G....................................$27.99

SONGS OF THE 2010s
All About That Bass • All of Me • Brave • Empire State of Mind • Get Lucky • Happy • Hey, Soul Sister • I Knew You Were Trouble • Just the Way You Are • Need You Now • Pompeii • Radioactive • Rolling in the Deep • Shake It Off • Shut up and Dance • Stay with Me • Take Me to Church • Thinking Out Loud • Uptown Funk • and many more.
00151836 P/V/G....................................$27.99

halleonard.com
Prices, content, and availability subject to change without notice.

CONTEMPORARY HITS
FOR PIANO, VOICE AND GUITAR

40 MOST STREAMED SONGS OF 2017-2018
40 of the Internet's most popular songs arranged for piano, voice and guitar. Includes: Despacito (Luis Fonsi & Daddy Yankee feat. Justin Bieber) • Feel It Still (Portugal. The Man) • New Rules (Dua Lipa) • Perfect (Ed Sheeran) • Wolves (Selena Gomez & Marshmello) • Young, Dumb and Broke (Khalid) • and more.
00283644 .... $19.99

CHART HITS OF 2019-2020
18 top singles arranged for piano and voice with guitar chords and lyrics. Songs include: Circles (Post Malone) • Dance Monkey (Tones and I) • Everything I Wanted (Billie Eilish) • Lose You to Love Me (Selena Gomez) • Lover (Taylor Swift) • Truth Hurts (Lizzo) • and more.
00334217 .... $17.99

Chart Hits of 2018-2019
18 of the hottest hits of '18 and '19, arranged for piano, voice and guitar. Includes: Eastside (Benny Blanco with Halsey & Khalid) • High Hopes (Panic! At the Disco) • Shallow (Lady Gaga & Bradley Cooper) • Sunflower (Post Malone & Swae Lee) • Without Me (Halsey) • and more.
00289816 .... $17.99

CONTEMPORARY R&B HITS
This collection pays tribute to two dozen of the best modern hits. Includes: All the Stars (Kendrick Lamar/SZA) • Girl on Fire (Alicia Keys/Nicki Minaj) • Love on the Brain (Rihanna) • Redbone (Childish Gambino) • and more.
00276001 .... $17.99

EDM SHEET MUSIC COLLECTION
37 hits from the EDM genre includes: Closer (The Chainsmokers feat. Halsey) • It Ain't Me (Kygo & Selena Gomez) • The Middle (Zedd, Maren Morris & Grey) • This Is What You Came For (Calvin Harris feat. Rihanna) • Titanium (David Guetta feat. Sia) • Wake Me Up! (Avicii) • and more.
00280949 .... $19.99

LATIN POP HITS
25 hot contemporary Latin songs including: Ahora Dice (Chris Jeday) • Bailando (Enrique Iglesias) • Despacito (Luis Fonsi & Daddy Yankee) • Échame La Culpa (Luis Fonsi & Demi Lovato) • Havana (Camila Cabello) • La Tortura (Shakira) • Súbeme La Radio (Enrique Iglesias) • and more.
00276076 .... $17.99

Order today from your favorite music retailer

Prices, contents, and availability subject to change without notice.

POP HITS
You get a lot of bang for your bucks with this great collection of 52 top pop hits for only $14.99! Features: Believer • Blank Space • Despacito • Fight Song • HandClap • Lost Boy • Love Yourself • The Middle • One Call Away • Say Something • Send My Love (To Your New Lover) • 24K Magic • Wake Me Up • and more.
00289154 .... $14.99

POPULAR SHEET MUSIC – 30 HITS FROM 2017-2019
Play your favorite contemporary hits with this collection. Includes 30 songs: Bad Liar • Good As Hell • Havana • If I Can't Have You • Lover • The Middle • New Rules • Shallow • Shape of You • Sucker • Without Me • You Are the Reason • and more.
00345915 .... $19.99

TOP HITS OF 2018
18 of the best from '18 are included in this collection for piano, voice and guitar. Includes: Delicate (Taylor Swift) • In My Blood (Shawn Mendes) • Let You Down (NF) • The Middle (Zedd, Maren Morris & Grey) • New Rules (Dua Lipa) • No Tears Left to Cry (Ariana Grande) • and more.
00283394 .... $17.99

TOP HITS OF 2019
20 of the year's best are included in this collection. Includes: Bad Guy (Billie Eilish) • Dancing with a Stranger (Sam Smith & Normani) • ME! (Taylor Swift feat. Brendon Urie) • Old Town Road (Remix) (Lil Nas X feat. Billy Ray Cyrus) • Senorita (Shawn Mendes & Camila Cabello) • 7 Rings (Ariana Grande) • and more.
00302271 .... $17.99